AMAZON

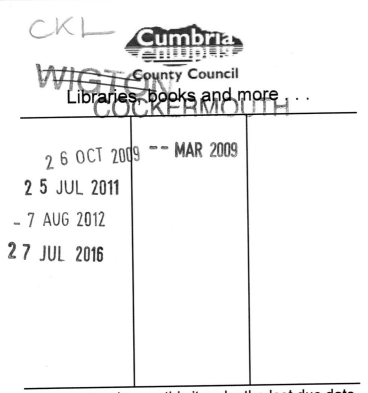

AMAZON

BRUCE PARRY

WITH JANE HOUSTON

PENGUIN

MICHAEL
JOSEPH

MICHAEL JOSEPH

Published by the Penguin Group
Penguin Books Ltd, 80 Strand, London WC2R 0RL, England
Penguin Group (USA) Inc., 375 Hudson Street, New York, New York 10014, USA
Penguin Group (Canada), 90 Eglinton Avenue East, Suite 700, Toronto, Ontario, Canada M4P 2Y3
(a division of Pearson Penguin Canada Inc.)
Penguin Ireland, 25 St Stephen's Green, Dublin 2, Ireland (a division of Penguin Books Ltd)
Penguin Group (Australia), 250 Camberwell Road, Camberwell, Victoria 3124, Australia
(a division of Pearson Australia Group Pty Ltd)
Penguin Books India Pvt Ltd, 11 Community Centre, Panchsheel Park, New Delhi – 110 017, India
Penguin Group (NZ), 67 Apollo Drive, Rosedale, North Shore 0632, New Zealand
(a division of Pearson New Zealand Ltd)
Penguin Books (South Africa) (Pty) Ltd, 24 Sturdee Avenue, Rosebank, Johannesburg 2196, South Africa

Penguin Books Ltd, Registered Offices: 80 Strand, London WC2R 0RL, England

www.penguin.com

First published 2008
1

Copyright © Indus Endeavour Ltd, 2008

Photography supplied by:
Marina de Boto: pp. 146, 164
Matt Brandon: pp. 19/20, 136/7, 138
Christina Daniels: pp. 212, 220, 223, 224, 227, 231, 232, 236, 237, 238/9, 240, 241, 242/3, 249
Pete Eason: pp. 1, 78/9, 89, 95, 106(2), 108/9, 112/3, 114/5, 118, 121, 125, 126, 128/9, 131, 254/255
Almudena Garcia-Parrado Gomez-Lobo: pp. 42(2), 48/9, 51, 65
Heron Alencar: pp. 219, 220, 227, 228, 229, 231, 232, 234/5, 244, 246/7
Ollie Laker: pp. 209/10, 211
Willow Murton: pp. 5, 6/7, 54, 62(2), 65, 70, 71, 72/3,
74, 77, 82/3, 85, 86/7, 91, 250, 252/3 and jacket image
Laura Santana: pp. 117, 122(2)
Zubin Sarosh: pp. 10, 14/15, 16/17, 19, 22, 26, 28/9, 32/3, 34/5, 36, 40/1,
45, 46, 51, 56/7, 60/61, 66/7, 70, 134/5, 144/5, 146, 148/9, 151, 152/3, 156,
157, 158/9, 162/3, 166, 168/9, 176/7, 178/9, p.180/1, 186, 192/3, 195, 197,
198/9, 200, 201, 202/3, 204, 207
James Smith: p. 175; Rob Sullivan: p. 219
Leticia Valverdes: pp. 96/7, 99, 100/1, 103 104/5, 143(2),
154(2), 161, 167, 186(2), 191(2), 195, 196

The moral right of the author has been asserted

Printed in Italy by Printer Trento
Colour Reproduction by Dot Gradations Ltd

A CIP catalogue record for this book is available from the British Library

ISBN: 978-0-718-15434-9

FSC
Mixed Sources
Product group from well-managed
forests and other controlled sources
Cert no. CQ-COC-000012
www.fsc.org
© 1996 Forest Stewardship Council

To all those who are trying to help save the Amazon

CONTENTS

VENEZUELA
GUYANA
COLOMBIA
ECUADOR
Andoas
Wijint
Iquitos
Jarauá
Manaus
Atalaia
Tabatinga
Benjamin Constant
Aurelio
Grota Rica
Paraná
PERU
Catunga
Luisana
Abancay
Nevado Mismi
BOLIVIA

SURINAME

FRENCH
GUIANA

Belém

Santarém

Altamira

BRAZIL

INTRODUCTION
SOURCE TO SEA

The Amazon is the world's biggest river system and its forest contains more species than found anywhere else on the entire planet. It's a vital part of the global ecosystem, but it's also home to millions of people. Every politician and environmentalist has got an opinion on the Amazon but Bruce Parry and the team behind *Tribe* set out to hear the voices of the Amazon people themselves, from indigenous tribes deep in the rainforest to cattle ranchers at the ever-moving forest edge, and to show the Amazon as it is now, with all its conflicts and complications.

Bruce would travel from the source in the Andes to the Atlantic coast, using the river as a route through the forest. Along his way he would live with the different communities he encountered — he would hunt caimans with riverside fishermen, collect coca leaf with impoverished farmers and pick up tools in illegal gold mines. By living and working alongside the people of the Amazon, Bruce would meet the families that depend upon the forest for survival and uncover the human stories from the environmental frontier.

The resulting television programme and this book aren't an answer to the conflicts on the environmental front line. But they are an honest portrayal of the people of Bruce Parry's journey along the Amazon, from source to sea.

'The stories within the Amazon are complex and important, those of human lives affected by big-headline issues: Cocaine, Oil, Logging, Gold.'

CHAPTER 1

COCA

In October of 2007 adventurer Bruce Parry and a small film crew set off on a journey through the Amazon basin. Their route is to roughly follow the course of the Amazon, using the river as a guide through the continent and discovering the stories of people living on its banks and tributaries.

The journey begins at the source of the Amazon, some 6,800 kilometres from the Atlantic, an icy trickle that subsequently forms the world's largest river. Bruce follows the river through Peru, along the tributaries of the upper reaches of the Amazon, travelling from the Andes Mountains into the Amazon rainforest.

In its entirety, this rainforest covers seven million square kilometres and is home to the planet's greatest biodiversity: a square kilometre contains thousands of tonnes of living plants. The rainforest helps regulate the balance of atmospheric carbon dioxide and oxygen; but it's under threat. At the current rates of deforestation, half of the Amazon forest could be lost by 2050.

In Peru, Bruce is to find that the stories of the people and their environment were affected by one plant in particular: the coca leaf. At the source, Quechua-speaking llama herders use coca leaf in rituals invoking Inca deities: a legal use of the leaf that links the people of South American highlands with a pre-Spanish past.

Downriver, the purposes of the leaf become more illicit. In Peru, growing and using unaltered coca leaf is permissible but any process that converts the leaf into the base substance for cocaine is illegal. In the notorious Red Zone around the last

stretch of the Río Apurímac and along the Río Ene, some farmers cultivate coca. A portion of their harvest is sold legitimately and the rest is sold illegally, where it is then refined into cocaine destined for the international drug market. As a result, the US Drug Enforcement Administration and the Peruvian Narcotics Police have a visible armed presence in the area.

ABOVE: Views from Nevado Mismi, near the source of the Amazon, where Bruce begins his adventure

Also along the Río Ene live the Asháninka, the largest indigenous group in the Peruvian Amazon. The total indigenous population of the Amazon basin is estimated to be around 700,000 people, in over 230 ethnic groups. In common with other tribes of the Amazon, the Asháninka are often witnessing the disappearance of the forest that is their home; sixteen per cent of the Amazon rainforest has already gone for ever.

The Asháninka are also still suffering the effects of the bloody civil unrest between the Shining Path and the Peruvian army in the 1980s and 90s. The Shining Path is a radical Maoist militia, founded with an avowed aim to overthrow the existing order and create a perfect communist state in Peru. Around the Río Ene, anti-Shining Path patrols formed in opposition and rebel brutality was met by state or state-sponsored repression. A commission by the government of Brazil found that around 70,000 people died in the insurgency between 1980 and 2000.

A few years ago, after the violence of the Shining Path, the Asháninka succeeded in getting a legal title to a portion of their land; but they have little control over the majority of their forest home, which is often under threat from encroaching coca farmers, loggers and oil companies. They're at the frontline of an environmental conflict that is relevant to the entire globe.

18 October. Heathrow

I'm in the departure lounge at Heathrow airport, setting off on a six-month trip to follow the Amazon from its source in the High Andes to the Atlantic coast in Brazil, where it releases a torrent of fresh water miles out into the ocean. I was on the road for three years making *Tribe*, and now I'm back travelling after a few months' break at home.

We've checked about fifty bags through customs – including a portable crane, countless cameras and a case full of medical equipment. On *Tribe* there was just a director, a cameraman and me – now we have a crew of six and a huge budget. There have been months of furious preparation. We will be filming in the most biodiverse region on earth, with some of the last uncontacted tribes, and we need all this equipment and expertise to do it as well as we can.

Amazon will be a new challenge for me in front of the camera. Unlike *Tribe*, I won't be staying in any one community for a long time to immerse myself in their culture. Instead we'll be constantly journeying: this isn't an expedition in the sense that we'll march along the Amazon, but we will use the river as a rough route through the continent to tell the stories of the different people that depend upon it.

Sometimes I will live with Amazonian tribes, but we plan to add more context than on *Tribe*, by showing the threats to the tribes and their environment. I will spend time with the farmers, ranchers and gold miners of the Amazon, and share their culture in the same way as with the tribes we visit. We want to try to understand all sides of the story and to show it as objectively as possible.

The stories within the Amazon are complex and important, those of human lives affected by big-headline issues: the cocaine trade, logging and slavery. They're stories important to the people and tribes of the Amazon; to Peru and to the rest of the world too, which is in itself a contentious issue.

It's an exciting and intimidating challenge, and it will begin after an eighteen-hour flight to Peru – I'm sure Heathrow departure lounge will soon seem a million miles away.

24 October. Colca

I'm sitting in blazing sunshine in a place called Colca in the High Andes. We've been in Peru now for about four days after flying to Cusco, a city in the southeast of the country, with the whole team. The crew are Matt Brandon (producer/director) and Matt Norman (cameraman), both of whom I worked with on *Tribe* in Tanzania. Then there's Zubin, our sound recordist, and Almu, our assistant producer. I haven't worked with either of them before.

Cusco was the perfect place for us to rendezvous and finalize our plans for the trip. The Ancient Incas knew Cusco as 'the centre of the universe' and it's full of monumental Catholic architecture built over the sites of old Inca temples destroyed when the conquistadors came to the High Andes. Perhaps it's symbolic of the mix of cultures in Andean religion and life.

We're going to acclimatize here at Colca Lodge before we head up to the source of the Amazon. We're at an altitude of about 3,500 metres here and I can feel the effects as soon as I start to do anything energetic. The source is higher again – higher even than Everest Base Camp – so it's important we try to accustom our bodies to the lack of oxygen.

26 October. Mismi

We have started. We're at the source, on a mountain called the Nevado Mismi, and filming has finally begun. Up here the landscape seems barren, almost lunar at times – a vista of parched brown and dusty grey against a bright blue sky.

We walked here over dry, stony ground where the wind builds the dust up and piles it round your boots, so you trek through it like snow. Most of the crew have been chewing coca leaves – the local remedy for altitude sickness, you wrap it up with charcoal, which acts as a catalyst to release the cocaine, to help your body deal with the reduced oxygen absorption at altitude. Inca culture has used coca leaf like this since ancient times and as the source itself is just under 5,200 metres, it's at a pretty extreme altitude. Everyone's suffering from nausea, headaches and an inability to sleep – you wake up gasping, unable to get enough oxygen. So I'm up for taking anything that can help.

The source itself is inspiring. The water literally pours out of a cliff face – spurts of the cold crystal liquid gush out of the rock. There's something elemental, mysterious and exciting about the place: this spring of water is the start of the world's biggest river. David, our interpreter, performed a coca leaf ceremony: he placed coca leaves in the water while invoking the Inca deities. It seemed very fitting, not in a religious way, but taking part in this ritual seemed to symbolically connect us to something ancient that had taken place in this landscape.

27 October. Rodolfo's estancia

It's night-time in Rodolfo's estancia. We arrived yesterday evening, meeting our family of llama herders in the dark as they waited for me outside their hut. Rodolfo lives close to the source of the Amazon, so his home is the ideal start for our journey.

LEFT: It has long been known that the source of the Amazon is from an Andean glacier, and in 2000 a National Geographic expedition pinpointed the source to this spring on Nevado Mismi

PREVIOUS PAGE: Matt Norman, Zubin and Almu filming the Andean mountains around the source

I could tell instantly how kind and generous Rodolfo and his family were. He has an obvious intelligence and a ready smile, which has been raised often by my attempts this evening at Spanish and Quechua. Soon the crew ducked out and left me with the family. It's always weird for me when the crew depart: I'm reluctant to see them go, which must be due to some comfort factor, but then when they leave I'm always happier. I like interacting with people on my own terms and my experience tonight was no exception. Once I'd got past the initial stumbling, almost embarrassed moments of conversation, and managed to make fun of myself a bit, everyone relaxed. It is a very special thing to be welcomed into someone's home and family, to sleep and to eat with them. We ate alpaca soup and I think I managed to convey my heartfelt thanks to Rodolfo.

28 October. Rodolfo's estancia

It's evening and I've been making doughnuts with the family. The crew left a while ago after a busy day of preparation for our two-day walk over the mountains with Rodolfo and his llamas. We'll be following the course of the river from its source, along a mountain pass used since Inca times. I've spent the day learning how to use a slingshot and to harness a llama, and I showed Rodolfo's family some *Tom and Jerry* on my iPod, which three-year-old Icka in particular found highly amusing. He screamed for more, then ran off and punched his dad!

It's been great getting to know this family and experiencing their customs. Today a sheep was slaughtered ceremoniously, during which various Incan deities were invoked. The family also conducted a ritual with coca leaf to mark the start of my journey, in which they called upon Pachamama to confer her blessing – Pachamama is an Inca deity comparable to a Mother Earth figure. As far as I could tell, there were no Christian references in these rituals, although the family here are devoutly Catholic.

The family have given me a poncho, and I discovered it's the one that Gladis, Rodolfo's wife, wove for him for their wedding day. They don't have rings here, so a wedding poncho is pretty important. Rodolfo, however, was presented with another poncho on the day, which he chose to wear, so they've been waiting to find the right person to whom to give this one. It's a huge honour that I am that lucky person.

In monetary terms, I've come to realize just how poor the family are: their income derives from their alpaca fleeces, which are sold for virtually nothing, so they augment this further by selling dung. They make about US$2,000 a year and half

of that goes on their daughter's university education, of which they are immensely proud. So when I found out they'd bought me a Stetson and a scarf, it showed a level of generosity that was hard to bear.

30 October. Angostura

We've just finished walking across the mountains with Rodolfo and his family. Little Icka was tied on to a donkey, and the llamas were loaded up with our kit, wearing bells that rang and with flags and blankets flapping all over the place in the wind. That morning we woke to a coating of snow over the Andes and the brightly coloured ponchos and flags stood out against the expanses of white. Despite the altitude I felt great. Rodolfo and his family were as appreciative of the beauty of the Andes as I was, and we were all bursting with energy and excitement. My day was plagued, however, by bad guts, which impeded my journey because I had to stop frequently to hide behind rocks and relieve my explosive bowels.

We're now spending our final night with Rodolfo and his family – I'm already sad that we'll be saying goodbye to them tomorrow morning. We've pitched our tents by the Río Apurímac, alongside a stunning escarpment that marks the start of the canyon. This evening producer Matt and I need to thrash out the final details of the huge trek along the river that I'll be making tomorrow, which will be the first physical challenge of this expedition: I'm intending to trek about forty kilometres and we still have to figure out how we'll fit everything in and get to where we need to be by nightfall – it's a tight schedule.

2 November. Cusco

Evening time in Cusco, and we're back here after three physically demanding days that included two days of kayaking, a forty-kilometre trek and one emotional goodbye. I'll start in reverse order . . .

We left Rodolfo and his family on Halloween morning. I really wanted to reciprocate their generosity, ideally by giving him my puffa jacket because he'd given me his poncho – but it would have been foolish to risk getting stuck without warm clothing. So I gave him my boots instead, as he had often asked me about them. To the family, we gave a male alpaca, which hopefully they will be able to mate with another alpaca of theirs that I had named Mismi.

The trek started with a cold wade through the river. I was walking with John, our fixer, and we were to meet the crew later at a place called Tres Cañones. We had

a glorious solitary day. John prefers to navigate by reading the land and following his nose, which is a style I really like. We came across few people, who mostly ran away or hid, and we missed the path on occasions but always returned to it, finding our way back to the river.

PREVIOUS PAGE: Bruce and Rodolfo take a pause while trekking along an ancient Inca route in the Andes. High altitudes make physical activity difficult, particularly for those unaccustomed to the lack of oxygen

The next day I was on the river with Eric – a Peruvian canoeing champion. I'd only ever done one day's white water in my life, in North Wales, and that was seventeen years ago. Eric gave me a quick lesson with a few useful tips: how to lean into rocks and come in and out of eddies. And then we were off down the river, which is the Apurímac at this point but after a series of confluences becomes the Amazon. I was on a real high because this was no longer a stream out of a rock but a fast-flowing river down a canyon, and it was thrilling to picture it becoming the huge Amazon River I've seen snaking through the rainforest in countless aerial photographs.

Today started on the water again, or should I say *in* it, as after about a minute I flipped my kayak, an instant reminder that I needed to rein in my confidence. We stopped at Machu Puente, a village near Eric's hacienda, to observe the Day of the Dead, an ancestral celebration observed across Latin America. The village itself was a ghost town because it had been abandoned in the 1940s after an outbreak of illness; the only thing in use was the church graveyard where the celebration was underway. All the graves had been cleaned up and many had fresh flowers. Plastic sheeting had been erected around some of them and within that space people were performing ceremonies. The Day of the Dead is a chance not only to remember your loved ones, but also to re-enact a part of the life you shared with them, so specific artefacts are brought that were important to the deceased, while food is symbolically shared with the souls of the dead.

There was a lot going on. I tried to give a piece to camera explaining the importance of the ceremony, but it soon became apparent that most of the people we were filming were pretty drunk, particularly one tiny old lady in a black hat who was intent upon holding my hand and dragging me around the graveyard. We joined a picnic in the cemetery but I really needed to vomit, probably a result of three days of continued physical activity coupled with a day or so of churning guts. I managed a small amount of bread and potatoes and then we set off on a pretty rough six-hour journey back to Cusco, where I am presently nursing my stomach and looking forward to getting back on the river in a day or so – this time in a raft.

5 November. Abancay

The last two days have been complete and unadulterated fun. The crew and I have been rafting down the Apurímac and it's been great: glorious sunshine, condors soaring above and an exciting challenge. It's been like having the best holiday ever. I love this river.

8 November. Luisiana

We've broken the first rule of this, our most dangerous phase of the expedition, which is never to arrive after dark. We're on our way to the Apurímac valley. A risky area where the narcotics industry and the Peruvian authorities are engaged in a continuous power struggle. We stopped for lunch on the way at a settlement where a few days previously a rocket-propelled grenade had hit the police post – killing the head of police and injuring others – reputedly as a result of a narcotics vendetta.

That evening there was a beautiful red sunset as we came across some police dangling AK-47s out the side of their vehicles. We pulled up and asked if there were any problems on the way and were told that we could certainly encounter some, before the police zoomed off in the opposite direction. It's an indication of the type of area we're entering – a rarely visited place with a reputation for lawlessness.

Today's journey was from Ayacucho to Luisiana, again a long haul of a drive that we were lucky to complete at all: the area around Ayacucho was beset with strikes by trade unions and the coca leaf growers (known as *cocaleros*) who are unhappy with the restrictions placed upon the agriculture of coca. Strikes in this area often cause roadblocks for days or even weeks, so we were fortunate not to be stopped. On the way we picked up Pepe Parodi, an old guy who was returning to his farm for the first time in eighteen years. He is an ex-local governor of the area and we are going to stay at his hacienda in the Red Zone. We travelled along the eastern edge of the Andes with Pepe, where Inca ruins stand on the slopes in almost impenetrably thick cloud, and he told us his story.

This was one of only a few times he had returned to his family farmstead since the Shining Path, a Maoist insurgent group, had razed the place thirty years ago. It was the first time he and his wife would be there together. This was particulary poignant as she had only just escaped the raid by hiding in the sugar cane until he'd rescued her.

A man called Gusman, now imprisoned for life, set up the Shining Path more than thirty years ago. In the Ayacucho region he and his followers attempted to restructure society according to strict Maoist principles. They came into the area and, later, using extreme violence, threatened the Andean lowland farmers to be either with them or against them. All the people of the local area were suddenly plunged into the midst of a bloody and terrible period in which the Shining Path and the state military vied for control using any means possible.

It's fascinating to meet Pepe, a real person behind the dreadful statistics of the violence, and speak with someone who survived but lost his livelihood and saw the destruction of the people and places he knew and loved.

9 November. Luisiana

We're at Luisiana hacienda and I've been wandering around barefoot on the grass, contemplating the challenge ahead. Over the next few days we will meet growers who harvest coca, and also people working in the labs to create coca paste, the first stage in the cocaine-making process. We're trying to show the story of the coca growers in an unbiased way, representing the views of the police, the *cocaleros* and the Asháninka – the tribe who live in this area.

I feel a huge responsibility to help Matt get in all these stories, and we both know that 90 per cent of what we film won't make the final cut. I'd never pretend to be an expert on these issues, but Matt and I have to make this story succinct and not dehumanize any aspect of it. All sides of narcotic production involve human stories and often tragic ones, but it's important for us both to leave our own preconceptions and judgements aside and try to portray what we find here.

9 November. Antonio's household

We drove up to the village of Santa Rosa yesterday afternoon to meet the coca growers. The village sits on the side of a ridge surrounded by jungle; it's derelict, with shacks made of wood and corrugated metal, dirty laundry on lines and people who are slow to smile.

As soon as we arrived I messed around with the kids. I was chucking myself about, making a fool of myself, and I think it softened a few hearts. Once everyone came back from the fields, Antonio, the village leader, called a meeting where I asked permission for us to film. I told the community I was on a journey and wanted to tell the stories of the people I met along the way. I explained that we thought the story of the coca growers is important, and one not often told. People were pleased that we were there and agreed to let us film – of the whole community, only one woman expressed any scepticism.

The crew went back before darkness fell, leaving me to stay with Antonio's family, on the floor of their mud hut. Antonio and his wife told me how they were

first displaced by the Shining Path. Antonio was fourteen when the conflict came to his village and he saw many people killed – often strung up or shot. Initially lots of the farmers were quite interested in the Shining Path and thought the communist doctrine seemed like a good idea. But he said that it was a badly led campaign that became one of terror and paranoia. The Shining Path murdered indiscriminately. People would turn in their neighbours for some petty vendetta and they'd be killed instantly. Everyone was caught up in the violence, and people like Antonio and his family had no choice but to pack a bag and flee in the night. There was massive displacement and thousands ran, terrified.

Next I asked about growing coca. He said he knew it could be illegal, which is why he sells half his crop to the government-approved buyer of coca leaf: this coca won't be turned into cocaine but used to make legal products like medicines. That way Antonio stays registered and keeps his nose clean; but even though he leads the community, he doesn't stipulate that others must do the same. The other half of his crop he sells unofficially, for twice the price to people who use the plant to produce cocaine for export. He's a peasant farmer who has very little cash and this is how he can afford an education for his children.

Antonio talked about other parts of the country where there has been indiscriminate spraying of crops with herbicide, which he explains would devastate his entire community. He says that if the military came in to conduct an eradication policy here, there would be a war. At this point Antonio looked at me levelly and said, 'I've seen the Shining Path. I've seen people killed left, right and centre, and we're not afraid of that. If they come here we will fight for our lives; we'll fight for our coca because this is how we feed our families.' I could see he meant it.

10 November. Luisiana

Back at Luisiana, which feels like a haven for us all now, returning after a day and night helping Antonio with his coca harvest. Many in the crew are tired and unwell: Zubin seems to have recovered from a tummy bug but Almu has now succumbed to it and Matt Norman has also been ill. Matt Brandon is suffering too – a headache and something with his back – so we're all feeling the effects of the trip.

The last two days have been very interesting. Antonio has a few hectares of coca, which he harvests four times a year, and I helped him with his harvest today. It's a relatively easy harvest but he has to use a lot of pesticide, which takes up much of his income, and he's convinced that US helicopters have dropped a fungus that is killing off his plants.

We had a great morning with him and his family, picking leaves and asking questions and then drying and rolling the leaves ready for collection. Antonio used to grow coffee too but the market slumped and he doesn't trust that it won't happen again, whereas coca is more stable. This particular harvest, his three-monthly yield, he'll sell for about US$300, and after labour and pesticide, he'll make a clear profit of about US$100, which is about the same price as a gram of cocaine in London. He's hardly a bloody glamorous drugs baron.

22 November. Lima

I've left this diary for over a week because everything's been up in the air.

The day we came back from the coca fields Matt B.'s headache worsened. He'd slept during the afternoon at the hacienda while we all got on with other stuff. Then the next thing I knew, he was brought to me, one person on either side half dragging, half carrying him. He was unresponsive. Almu called the emergency services and handed me the phone while I examined Matt – he wasn't talking, his eyes were rolling; he was all over the place, and only responded to pain or light. He was very ill.

We spent a difficult night looking after Matt because it was too late in the day to evacuate him – it was dark and no plane would come. Everyone worked hard to keep him hydrated and comfortable. He was very disturbed in the night and didn't engage with anything at all. We all just fed him water from test tubes; it was extremely harrowing.

At first light American helicopters came from Palma Pampa and I sent Almu, Zubin and a local doctor with Matt; in a short time an aeroplane picked them up and flew them over the Andes to Lima. There a doctor met them with an ambulance and took Matt to a clinic, where he still is now.

The entire crew has been devastated – Almu and Zubin were in Lima, and Matt's family flew out with people from the production team in Cardiff. Matt Norman and I stayed in Luisiana for one more day before joining the rest of the crew in Lima; we spent the day filming because we didn't know if we'd ever be coming back, and we needed to visit a base lab – known as a *bossa* – to complete our cocaine story.

The *bossa* is an illegal coca lab in the jungle where coca leaves are turned into coca paste. We watched two guys mash coca leaves in bleach and water, then smash the hell out of the leaves by stamping on them for hours in a large tray. Next they put the leaves in drums and mixed in kerosene and hydrochloric acid, then they reduced the water from the mixture.

They don't make much money – about $100 in four days between two people – and they'd go to jail for about five years if they were caught. While they were making the paste a helicopter flew overhead and we all hid under tree-cover in case it was the Drug Enforcement Administration or the Peruvian military. It was a strange day for Matt N. and me: we were both thinking of Matt B.'s illness all day. Early the following morning we flew to Lima to be with him.

23 November. Palma Pampa

Matt is now making an amazing and dramatic recovery from a brain abscess. He's still in intensive care in Lima with his family, but he's due to fly back to the UK as soon as possible. This last week in Lima was different and weird; the team were incredibly busy trying to assess what had happened, how effective our response had been, and how we could continue with the film.

Steve Robinson, the series producer of *Amazon*, has come out to take Matt's place and so we're picking up the pieces and carrying on with exactly the same team minus Matt. (There's obviously a whole load more detail about this week, and the effect that Matt's illness had on us all personally and on the production, but it's his story to tell so I won't dwell on it here. The most important thing is that he's making a full recovery.)

We've returned to Palma Pampa – to start where we left off – and attempt to go on a raid with the American backed Peruvian Narcotics Police.

The camp commandant had agreed that if they find a *bossa*, they would come and take us to film them blowing it up. While we waited at their base, we watched the police receiving their brief – a PowerPoint presentation and grid references for the locations they would visit. They then had half an hour off. A cynic would assume that it would be possible for these guys to get on the phone to any of their friends at that location. I spoke with the Peruvian commandant and a representative from the US Special Forces, both of whom were eloquent and charming. They seemed to suggest that all they were doing was making cocaine production a little more difficult to achieve, and that this approach wouldn't really stop the problem: the *bossas* are pretty cheap and easy to rebuild.

We got the call that a *bossa* had been found, so I jumped into the back of the patrol vehicle with the police and their heavy machine guns and we drove through the villages. I wanted to wave at everyone but felt that would be a bit incongruous. People simply ignored us, which shows how routine these operations are.

When we arrived at the target, a helicopter was charging around overhead

and on the radio a warning came through that a load of people in a pick-up were heading straight for us. It didn't amount to anything, it was just a typical military technique of covering the unit, but it highlighted the nature of the situation the police face here – they do encounter extremely violent reactions to what they are doing, they do get shot at, and they do get killed.

When we arrived at the *bossa* I found myself in an awkward situation: I didn't let on to the commandant that I'd seen one before, not wanting to implicate the people I'd been with previously. I had to ask a series of innocent questions, whereas in reality I'd already seen the whole set-up in operation at the other lab. No one was there when we arrived and the police set the whole thing alight.

25 November. Catunga

I'm in my tent with little chance of sleep because there is incredibly loud music blaring out of a huge amp nearby. I'm in a village called Catunga, where we arrived yesterday to stay with the Asháninka tribe. We travelled by boat to Shioteri, a settlement on the Río Ene, and then drove to Catunga. Two trucks filled with booze and a cow kept bumping into us.

When we arrived we encountered a huge celebration to mark the twelfth anniversary of the village. The houses, made of ugly planks of roughly sawn wood, were covered in bunting and there was a huge banner.

The following morning we held a meeting with the community to explain our presence. They have an understandable fear of outsiders and we needed to prove we weren't there to steal their oil and wood. When they asked what we could give them, I answered very carefully that we could provide an opportunity for them to talk to the world on camera. I have to be very honest when I tell people what we can give them: it is unethical to promise too much.

A lot of people at the meeting were reluctant to talk, and it dawned on me that there were many outsiders present, people not from this community but from Porto Ene, the nearby town. These people's interests are often in conflict with those of the Asháninka. They're farmers from the Andes, *cocaleros* and loggers, and they all have competing claims to the land that the Asháninka call their own. They're here ostensibly to join in the festivities, but potentially to infiltrate the community.

I told them all how we'd heard about the *ronderos* (patrols) they make to protect their land and that we wished to show their situation honestly. Immediately they started to open up and talk about their problems. I told them that their side of

LEFT: Bruce at the *bossa*, an illegal coca lab in the jungle. It has just been set alight by the Peruvian Narcotics Police

PREVIOUS PAGE: Bruce travels with the Narcotics Police to a hidden *bossa*. Operations to destroy *bossas* are routine in this area but have a limited impact as the *bossas* are simple and cheap to rebuild

the story would be captured on camera over the next few days and then we could show it to people – and they agreed and granted us permission to film.

Next, two things happened: we were told we needed to enter a team into the football competition; and Ruth, our contact and fixer, arrived. Ruth is a wonderful woman, only thirty and pregnant with her third child. She is very important in this region, as she's not afraid to say what she wants and has stood up for the rights of the Asháninka in many different locations throughout Peru. She is extraordinarily charismatic and a true leader in this troubled part of the world.

The football wasn't so inspiring. I'm not sure if it's the best way to meet the villagers by knocking them over on the football pitch, but that's what happened. We lost all our matches and didn't score a goal and I ended up with a raised bruise on my shin that looked like a discoloured golf ball protruding from my leg.

In the evening a brilliant band played, but as I write it has unfortunately been replaced by the appalling cheap CD now blaring around the village and likely to continue until morning.

26 November. Catunga

Somehow I managed to sleep last night but I think I was the only one. It's apparent that we aren't going to get a massive amount done, as the majority of the village is either hungover or still drinking.

I'd hoped to go on a trek around the surrounding land but it wasn't possible. We were really honest about our intentions yesterday and some outsiders who were at the meeting have threatened the Asháninka as a result. They warned them that if the Asháninka took us to areas that these outsiders claim is land stolen from them, there would be violence, whether or not white people with cameras were there. The reason that we had avoided Porto Ene on the way here was to keep from alerting the *cocaleros* and farmers to our presence, so that we could get the story of the Asháninka without them being coerced by others. But the cat's out of the bag now, and we can't do the filming that we would like as it would endanger everyone.

We made a tiny patrol of the area but it was a bit of a farce: there was no path and it was difficult for poor Matt who, with his huge camera, didn't have a hope of keeping up.

On our return we tried *masato*, the Asháninka beer: it's made of yucca that they've masticated and then spat out; it's fizzy and bitter but surprisingly tasty. While we were drinking I asked the community leaders if our presence was putting anyone in danger and three people nodded at the same time. Later they retracted

this and told us to stay, but Steve and I both thought their initial response was honest and that we should trust it. It was too late to leave there and then but we decided to go at first light tomorrow.

It's a huge shame and it illustrates the continued threats the Asháninka face: from the farmers, the Shining Path and the *cocaleros*. As a group their rights are always over-shadowed by the demands of others. Don Pepe and Guillermo, the farmers at Luisiana, referred to them as *Kampa*, a derogatory word for the Asháninka; it's thought to come from the Quechua for 'ragged' or 'dirty', and it's considered offensive.

In addition to the danger posed by the farmers, they're threatened by the *cocaleros*. Coca requires a lot of nutrients to grow and after a while renders the land useless, and so the coca farmers need to encroach more and more on to the Asháninka lands.

Culturally, they're in a huge state of flux. Everything we've seen here – the football, the pop group, the wood houses, the bunting – it's all imported from elsewhere. They're struggling with their groups of *ronderos*; they're trying to protect themselves. Perhaps this isn't surprising, given their recent history. The Shining Path was very destructive for the Asháninka: they literally stole their children from them. The Truth and Reconciliation Commission in Peru found that during the Shining Path era 10,000 Asháninka were displaced, 6,000 died, 5,000 were taken captive and between 30 and 40 communities disappeared. Ruth speaks with personal knowledge about the difficulties of this time: she lost her own father to the Shining Path.

The fight to keep their land is bloody and difficult, and it's right in their back garden.

27 November. Pamakiari

We left the community at Catunga this morning and took a boat downstream from Shioteri to another Asháninka village, Pamakiari. It's very beautiful, with gardens and thatched roofs, surrounded by fields used for swidden (slash and burn) agriculture. Ruth, who is still with us, explained the origins of this settlement. Previously the Asháninka were semi-nomadic farmers, who moved around in small family units, but over the last century they've brought themselves together into larger settled groups for protection, most recently due to the threat from the Shining Path.

As the Asháninka don't have a tradition of confrontation and debate, when there have been conflicts within the community people have just moved away from the main settlement and established satellite communities. Other potential leaders, rather than confronting problems, have moved away to establish these smaller communities.

LEFT: Bruce wearing Asháninka dress in the satellite community of Pamakiari. The red dye on his face is made from seeds of the urukum palm, used as a pigment across the Amazon.

29 November. Pamakiari

RIGHT: A young Asháninka woman holding a child. The future of the Asháninka depends on a difficult struggle to keep their land and communities intact in the face of external pressures

BELOW: Ruth, an inspirational advocate for the Asháninka and their rights

PREVIOUS PAGE: Bruce is welcomed into the Asháninka community of Pamakiari, which felt like a sanctuary for the team after the difficulties they had experienced along the Ene valley

This is our last night in the village and we've had a lovely two days. Everyone here has been pleased to see us and we've been greeted wholeheartedly as friends, but there is nothing like the relationships that would develop on *Tribe*.

Last night we showed a load of *Tribe* films to the community on our computers and they loved watching them, but it made me reflect on the differences between the programmes. On *Tribe* we'd spend a good while getting to know people before I even started to participate with the community, but there isn't the time on this trip, particularly because we needed to move on from the last village so quickly.

Some elements of the film will be similar to *Tribe*: for example, I went hunting today with Walter, the chief, who was armed with a shotgun. We caught an armadillo, which Walter shot a couple of times – the poor thing was bouncing about all over the place in a load of pain. We trekked home with it and I almost walked into a snake at head height. It was about a metre long with a small mouth and I think it was a coral snake, which is pretty dangerous. I was also hunted myself – by insects: I wasn't wearing mosquito repellent because animals smell it and it spoils the hunt.

It's easy to give an over-romanticized view of tribal communities, but today I was reminded of our cultural differences from the Asháninka. A baby in the community was very ill, and we discovered his family had abandoned him as they already had six sons. Another family had taken in the infant, but nobody would breastfeed it because people thought it was bewitched. He was a year old but was tiny and looked far younger. Chris, our team doctor, with us since Matt's illness, did his best with nutrients and medicine but we're not sure the boy will survive. The child's father is also the assigned medic in the community, so it was with him that we had to leave the medicines. It was strange for us but it is neither my place nor policy to take the moral high ground.

1 December. Atalaya

Film 1 is finished. We left the Asháninka and I bade a fond farewell to Ruth. She does so much for this area and cares hugely for the Asháninka, but she will have to step down from some of her roles to care for her family. Who knows what the future holds for the Asháninka? After decades of terrorism, civil war, logging and cocaine growing they've already had the roughest of rides. Sadly, now much of their land is under scrutiny for oil exploration, and I fear their troubles are far from over. Oil is also going to be at the heart of the next shoot, as we're travelling further into the jungle to where the petrol industry threatens another indigenous group – the Achuar.

'Oily petrolem was floating into the rivulets like black poison, and we followed the stream to the river, from which Guevara, his family and his neighbours drink, fish and wash.'

CHAPTER 2
SHAMANS & OIL

Bruce Parry's Amazonian adventure continues deeper into the Peruvian jungle, into the territories of the Achuar tribe. The Achuar live in rainforest that lies over billions of dollars' worth of oil. Bruce and the crew first visited a traditional community of hunters and their families on the Río Huitoyacu and then travelled to the Río Corrientes, where oil has been extracted for over thirty years. Here the Achuar have become accustomed to the presence of big industry.

Since it was first seen by Spanish colonists, the Amazon rainforest has been regarded as a wilderness packed with valuable resources. Oil was first discovered in the early twentieth century and the petrol industry is lucrative business in Peru. However, the Achuar view the rainforest differently. Rather than just seeing the forest as a bounty of goods to exploit, the forest is their home and they rely on their territory for hunting animals and gathering plants. But the forest isn't just a food-store: the Achuar consider that each plant and animal has its own spirit and consciousness. They seek to live harmoniously with these spirits by treating the forest with respect, and taking its resources only in moderation.

The Achuar consider the spirits important for their health and survival and they communicate with them through song, in dreams, and during rituals such as the ayahuasca ceremony, during which participants drink a brew with hallucinogenic properties. This has been used for hundreds of years by peoples of the western Amazon, and can provoke a state of altered consciousness in which it is thought possible to meet and talk with the spirits. For the Achuar, protecting the rainforest means they protect the spirits and they protect themselves.

Currently, indigenous people such as the Achuar have rights to eleven million hectares of rainforest in Peru. However, communities often find the plots they have been granted are restrictively small and indigenous people claim rights to three times more land. Also, a title to land is not ownership: it's not guaranteed to last for ever and the state retains the possession of forestry and underground resources. This means that in titled areas, as in most countries, the Achuar own some of what is above the soil but the Peruvian government own all of what is below, including the oil.

In the Corrientes region, oil extraction began in 1971 and at its peak there was a daily production of 115,000 barrels of crude oil. This brought a cash economy to the Achuar but the forest got sicker, and they did too. Toxic waste polluted the water, heavy metals contaminated the food chain and as a result the Achuar have dangerous levels of cadmium and lead in their blood, substances that can cause serious illness, including cancer and genetic deformities. Due to suggestions of negligent practice, the Achuar are bringing a court case against a petrol company in the US.

Drilling, explosions and explorations continue, with considerable efforts to expand petroleum operations into new areas of forest that are often the home to indigenous people. The first Achuar community visited by Bruce has resisted oil companies for the last ten years, but the state persists in overlapping oil lots with indigenous territories, and can legally force communities to surrender to the petroleum industry.

The battle of the Achuar with the oil companies is a conflict between indigenous lands and the national ownership of resources. It's a collision between two different ideas of the forest. Ultimately, it's a contest about who owns the Amazon and what should be done with it.

LEFT: Oil pouring into a rivulet of the Río Corrientes – an area of the Amazon where there has been oil extraction since the 1970s

PREVIOUS PAGE:

Touching down in a

light aircraft on the

edge of the Peruvian

jungle. Tropical

storms and

unpredictable engines

result in a sense of

relief at the end of a

successful flight over

the forest

3 December. San Lorenzo

Film 2 started in a light aircraft over the jungle of Peru. The plane was equipped with a huge door for free-fall parachuting. Matt sat filming me in front of the open door. First we flew over high ground with cloud cover but then the land flattened and we stayed low – only 100 metres off the canopy at points. We could see endless forest in all directions.

I tried to do a piece to camera describing the magnitude of the place: the forest was so flat you could see the curvature of the earth, and looking down I knew that whichever way any of the hundreds of rivers may be flowing, even if they were separated by hills or mountains, they would all eventually end up in the Amazon.

We're going to meet the Achuar, a tribe that live in the Peruvian and Ecuadorian Amazon. We're filming them in two regions of Peru: along the Río Huitoyacu and the Río Corrientes. The crew is the same but with the hugely welcome addition of Willow, my great friend from *Tribe*, who has already been in Peru for over a month, working furiously to set up Film 2. Also with us is Aliya, an anthropologist working on a mapping project with the Achuar, and Angel, our aptly named fixer.

Our plane touched down in San Lorenzo and we checked into our accommodation, which looks more like a prison than a hotel – and has inspired a few jokes about porridge. The electricity is out and in the dark we've had the safety brief that we do at the start of every film but we're all slightly fractious after all the weeks of constantly going over safety. The huge buzz we had at the source of the Amazon hasn't left us, but it has slowed down. We've all worked long days on the first film, had huge troubles reorganizing dates and locations after Matt's illness, had stuff stolen, and we've been obsessing about safety and contingency plans. We're not at a grinding halt but we're not elated. We need to bring up the mood again for this film.

4 December. Río Huitoyacu

Evening time on the banks of the Río Huitoyacu. Our boat has been far slower than we anticipated and we haven't got into Achuar territory despite a day of chugging along the river without stopping. We've pulled up on a bank-side settlement with an hour of daylight left and have been given permission to stay in the schoolhouse.

We're travelling with Jorge, who has just stood down as the president of the Peruvian organization for the Achuar. Jorge comes from the Achuar village of Wijint, where we will be filming for a few days. His father isn't Achuar and Jorge speaks Spanish in addition to the Achuar language. He dresses in an urban manner, with short hair and city trousers. During his presidency he visited the US and spoke at the UN; he's a

passionate and charismatic man, and he's dedicated to his community and people.

I helped put up hammocks in the schoolhouse and now darkness has fallen there are beautifully clear stars. We're all full of anticipation now, and there's a sense of excitement in the team. The whisky's been opened; Steve, Zubin and Willow are setting some perfect time-lapse pictures; and before I retreat to my hammock I'm going to check out the beautiful starry night.

5 December. Wijint

Today we've been on the go since 5 a.m. and our boats haven't stopped all day. There are lots of fallen logs in the river, which has caused us a bit of engine trouble and slowed us down, so we've pushed on travelling into the night, using a big torch to give our captain a beam to spot obstructions. The boat behind doesn't have such a strong light and couldn't keep up, so at one point we turned off the engine to wait for them. With the noise gone, we were suddenly drifting on the river with the night sounds of the jungle alive around us.

Finally we arrived in Wijint. It's late and there are few people around. The whole terrain of the village is bare, not a single bit of foliage underfoot. In the centre there's a big football pitch, and around that a bunch of perfectly thatched huts and a blue schoolhouse.

We don't have much food and have made our camp for the night with empty stomachs. We're hoping just to spend a couple of days here to pay respects and get our permissions and then move on to a smaller Achuar community to film.

7 December. Wijint

The two things that I'd heard about the Achuar before I started researching them were that they are very suspicious of outsiders and are also highly organized, and today the community at Wijint proved both with considerable aplomb.

We were called to a meeting in the community hall, which is a corrugated iron and concrete structure alongside the football pitch. Steve had decided that, despite its size, Wijint would be suitable for filming and this decision would save us precious time because we wouldn't have to travel further downriver. All we needed was an invitation to stay here with a family.

We were asked to enter the meeting at the back of the hall in single file. I went in first and we walked the length of the building to the front. It was completely empty except for eight or nine men sitting facing us on a bench: these were the elders – the *apu*. We sat in a row facing the *apu*; they stood up in a line abreast of

us and stepped towards us, holding weapons – either shotguns, spears or roughly sharpened sticks. First there was silence but then they shouted, wailed and pushed their weapons in our direction. It didn't involve physical contact but was obviously an aggressive martial ritual.

I tried to catch the eye of the guy opposite me; he was pretty old and wearing a traditional feathered headdress and red face paint. He gave me a slight smile as he continued shouting but then realized his mistake and resumed affecting his gruff look.

Once they sat they immediately asked me to explain our presence, so I stood up and asked their permission to stay in the village. Luckily, Willow had spent a week here before, in three days of solid meetings, so we were at the end of a lengthy process of getting their permission.

After I had spoken they stood up in turn and told us what they thought. First, the spokesman – confusingly, also called *El Apu* – stood. *El Apu* is the youngest of the *apu*, he is a Spanish speaker, and his role has arisen because the Achuar need someone who can represent their interests outside their communities. He wanted to check that we were there for the right reasons – that we weren't from an oil company, and that we wouldn't betray them. Others stood up and echoed his thoughts: one man, Saris, spoke at length; he was pretty scathing towards us. Saris said that underhand envoys have encroached upon their lands, and we needed to prove that our intentions were genuine.

To do this we each introduced ourselves, and I tried to assure the community that we came with good intentions. I said that although we couldn't offer any magic solutions, we could offer them a voice.

In the middle of the day we took a break and went to the secondary school, which is run by six nuns from a mission based in Colombia. The school's students held a presentation for us on the football pitch, with different age groups performing a dance each. The young children enacted the story of Mother Nature giving her daughter to the Achuar to teach them how to use plants such as manioc, cassava and plantains: a tiny kid with a massive axe chopped down a palm tree and his classmate sliced it down the middle with a machete so the others could act out taking grubs from the centre of the tree and drinking *masato*, the same fermented brew drunk by the Asháninka.

The girls wore extraordinary fluorescent colours, their beads clattering as they danced, and the boys banged the drums slightly out of time and played whistles.

Some of the teenage male dancers started the same aggressive greeting ritual that the *apu* had performed. They were much less threatening than the elders had been. The guy in front of me just couldn't get it right. Whenever everyone else stepped back he'd

LEFT and BELOW: Students at the school put on a display of traditional dances, but they are far less intimidating than their elders

PREVIOUS PAGE: Jorge, who has represented the Achuar at the UN, is comfortable wearing both the latest city styles and traditional Achuar dress, like this headdress of toucan and macaw feathers

step forwards and vice versa; his face was covered in beads of sweat and he seemed pretty panicky. I was trying to catch his eye with a supportive smile but he never looked up.

At the end I was asked to speak. I thanked the nuns and the children and told them the message that I'd got from their dances was that they were trying to fight off outside agents and preserve their culture, to which the nuns nodded sagely.

Returning to the longhouse, we finished off the meeting with a long conversation about where I might stay in the village. Steve had privately wanted Saris to host me, as he had been so reluctant to welcome us initially. Somehow the *apu* had intuited this and kept asking Saris what he thought, but he had concerns: there was a party on Thursday and he didn't know whether he'd be able to get drunk if I was there. To allay his worries, the *apu* explained that I wasn't there as a visitor but to muck in with the family. Once that was clear Saris came up to shake my hand, so by the end of today we've eventually been permitted to stay. I am, however, a little concerned it has all happened so quickly. During *Tribe* we would always let these decisions develop more slowly.

8 December. Wijint

I got up at about six this morning with a full stomach from the night before. Yesterday was Zubin's birthday and Willow had got together a bit of a birthday feast, with some peanuts, chocolates, a Milky Way and a soft gelatinous pudding that the nuns had made. Also a rather sad-looking birthday cake was produced, which had travelled all the way from Cardiff; we had some tins of sardines and frankfurters; and we cracked open a bottle of one-dollar champagne that we'd bought in San Lorenzo. It was like a gourmet meal for us! We all tucked in royally and sang 'Happy Birthday' in Spanish.

I headed over to Saris' house in high spirits but unfortunately, while we'd been tucking into our feast, he'd had some discussions with his daughters and they'd concluded that they didn't want me to move in. This is a real blow, particularly because during yesterday's conversations Saris's mood towards us had changed from grumpy mistrust to excited enthusiasm, and convincing him of our genuine intentions had felt like such a victory. It shows us how hard it is to replicate filming styles used in *Tribe* on such a tight schedule.

It's a real headache because we've already lost a lot of time: we're here far later than we expected and Willow has frantically reorganized everything, but we're in a bit of a dilemma as to where to turn. Steve, Willow and I batted it back and forth for hours: should we stay here? Move to another community? Find someone else to stay with? We're all feeling the pressure of lost time and budget.

ABOVE: The village
of Wijint. Extended
families live together
in longhouses that
are built entirely
using materials from
the forest

PREVIOUS PAGE:
Achuar children play
football whatever
the weather, through
blazing heat and
tropical storms

We wandered around the village looking for more houses and potential characters, and were introduced to a returning hunter with a dead spider monkey on his back. His wife was very bubbly and communicative, asking us to come and share spider monkey with them tomorrow. She started to skin it and was fine with us filming, so Steve ran for the camera and filmed a good sequence. All the time she was chatting to us openly, with her beautiful kids running about. She is the first woman that has spoken to me here; all the rest have run away as I approach.

Steve and I were both thinking what a great place this would be for me to stay but we're so scared of putting a foot wrong that we didn't dare ask. However, we have been invited to come back at three tomorrow morning to drink *wayus* with Mantu, the hunter.

Hopefully it's working out.

9 December. Wijint

Woke up at 2.30 a.m. to arrive at Mantu's house at three. I sat around the pot with the men, and started drinking: *wayus* is a hot infusion with bits of floating leaf, traditionally drunk early every morning by Achuar to induce vomiting and purge them of bad spirits.

The others had been up since two so I was a bit behind. I sipped away while we talked about the business of the day for a couple of hours. Noticeably, the women are very vocal at these meetings and it's well known that most decision making occurs before first light, despite the lengthy male-only meetings throughout the day.

Stepping outside to vomit, I was able to throw up straight away without even having to stick my fingers down my throat. After I'd puked about three or four times I used my little finger to tickle my gag reflex; I was able to chunder the remains perfectly and it wasn't at all unpleasant. Then I returned to the hut and drank strong *masato* – nothing sweet.

This afternoon we visited Saris and helped chop some logs for his fire. I found a tree and attempted to chop it down. I wasn't doing a great job; it was a bit of a mess and I was feeling really weak for some reason, quite dizzy, pouring with sweat and irritated by the prickly thorns on the tree. (Later today I was told that this was because I hadn't thrown up all the *wayus*.) I was stamping all over the thorns, feeling quite self-conscious with the camera rolling. Old Saris sat watching and grumbling about it all – what a great old boy!

After we'd chopped the trees down, we carried the logs back to Saris's house and started to lay the fire. The Achuar make fires by setting the logs like spokes of

a wheel with the fire at the centre and they push the logs into the fire as they burn. I didn't know this at the time, so I laid the logs down as I saw fit. Saris was looking grumpy and bemused. He told me I had put one of the logs the wrong way round and basically started ordering me about, while chuckling to himself the whole time. Of course he doesn't realize that strangers don't cook like this at home.

Mantu has invited me to move in – result!

11 December. Wijint

Started again at two-thirty in the morning to drink *wayus* at Mantu's house. We talked about fishing and vomited. The crew arrived later, ready to set off on a fishing trip.

Our trek to the river was along a boggy path and it was fairly arduous due to the amount of filming and fishing kit we needed to carry. I was attempting to negotiate half-submerged logs and waterways with a heavy camera and a basket of leaves strapped to my head – as a result I ended up spending half the time thigh deep in marshy water.

On arrival we pounded the leaf and put the mush into the rattan baskets, which the men then carried to the river strapped to their heads. We stood waist deep in the water with the baskets in front of us and with our hands we mixed up

the poison leaf and rotated the top of the basket rapidly – as if it was a steering wheel and we were frantically driving a downhill course. This sluiced the poison nicely into the river and we wandered downstream with harpoons aloft.

I managed to spear a fair few of the asphyxiated fish as they flapped on the surface, and we caught a load of different species as we wandered downriver. The kids dived into the water after the gasping fish, spearing them expertly, and everyone in the crew had huge grins on their faces, especially Zubin who was delighted with his fishing prowess. There was a ripple of alarm when a stingray kept surfacing and then disappeared. Knowing danger lurked underwater was unsettling and after an hour of treading gingerly I was pleased to finally harpoon it.

At the end we rejoined the crew on the bank and trekked back through the jungle; we were all on a real high from spending a day out in the forest. Along the path I heard a loud buzzing too late and found myself walking through a sizeable swarm of bees. I tried to alert the others as it was potentially perilous but fortunately it turned out their stings weren't too potent and we could all laugh it off. Willow was picking bees out of her hair an hour later and this evening we're all counting our stings – we all have a few each, with the exception of Matt, who as usual was protected by head-to-toe clothing.

12 December. Wijint

Today is a big day for Mantu's family: his son is getting his school results and the community are celebrating the end of the school year. I asked Mantu about the difference between his life and his son's. Mantu was abandoned by his own parents and had been raised by his grandparents; he didn't attend school and grew up naked.

I wondered if he had found it interesting to hear what his son told him from school, things like the earth travelling round the sun – but he said his son never told him anything.

For the celebration, Mantu wore his traditional headdress, for which he has shot about thirty toucans and macaws and arranged their yellow, black and red feathers along a headband. It was a personal celebration for the family so I tried not to intrude.

I spent the time today fasting in preparation for tomorrow's ayahuasca ceremony. Ayahuasca is a vine plant used in a medicinal brew by many peoples of the western Amazon, often inducing hallucinations.

14 December. Wijint

It's the day after the ayahuasca ceremony and I've just woken up in my hammock – strung up between the rafters of the hut that belongs to Jorge's grandmother. Around me some of the other men who took ayahuasca are still sleeping off its effects.

Yesterday morning two Achuar men and I collected the ayahuasca vine (*Banisteriopsis caapi*) near a meander in the river where grass grew up to our chests. There's about three or four vines growing in this area and we took one to leave the others growing, cutting it into short sections for carrying.

Back at the hut, we pounded the vine cuts with sticks and put them in a large pot of water on a fire. Meanwhile we banged an impressive split-log drum to inform the spirits of our intentions and bring them near for our visions.

Entire families came and went and we all drummed in a slow rhythm as the vine boiled down. A little more water was added to the pot occasionally and sometimes it overflowed.

Early on in the ceremony we sipped some of the liquid to awaken our insides, as at this stage the Achuar consider the vine spirit is alive and strong in the brew. As the sun was setting we were washed and the shaman lined up about twenty bowls.

The *apu* had a long stick with a bowl at the end of it, which they used like a ladle as they didn't want to get too close to the liquid. Both the brew and the vine are treated reverentially: even after the vine has been pounded and boiled it doesn't

LEFT: Boots drying after the fishing trip. Although Bruce and the crew started with top-of-the-range hiking boots, wellies proved the best footwear for the jungle, and soon became the boots of choice for the team

PREVIOUS PAGE: Bruce drinking *masato* during the fishing trip. *Masato* is made by masticating yucca plant and spitting out the remains to make a fermented drink

get thrown away but is placed on a specially erected platform, where it is left for weeks to dry in the sun.

From the ladles the shaman filled up most of the long line of bowls, reserving three to be filled from a separate, darker pot of ayahuasca. These three bowls were for me and the other two guys who'd helped make the brew, and all the other pots were for latecomers who'd decided to join.

Initially the people arriving drank as the three of us watched. First the shaman traversed the line and lifted the bowl in front of each person to his lips, and then he stood stationary by the pot. The men would get another bowl filled by the ladle and they'd bring it to the shaman standing by the pot: the shaman would hold their bowl while they drank in order to pass his power to the drinker. The shaman's job is dangerous because he can be weakened by one of the ayahuasca recipients taking away his vital force, but he told me his life is good and he's happy to die if that's his fate.

Each recipient vomited and then went back for more and the shaman kept this chaotic conveyer belt going on until the huge vat was gone and everyone had vomited all they could. Then they went to their families, drank water, and vomited more until their vomit was clear. There was a sea of sick flowing beneath everyone's feet – a quite extraordinary visual spectacle and auditory experience.

Eventually it was our turn. Because we were the three protagonists our bowls were huge. I drank the whole thing, managing to keep it down, but then felt myself starting to shake – either from nausea or from an excess of serotonin. I started the second bowl and vomited but the shaman returned it and I had to keep drinking and vomiting. I don't know how many bowls I had in total but I can't pretend it was a particularly pleasant experience. Next I drank and vomited copious amounts of water to clean up my insides.

The wonderful thing about it all was that I finally experienced a true bond with Mantu, who kept giving me water. I felt a huge level of care and affection from this stoical hunter as he checked my pulse and temperature. To get a vision I needed to rest in my hammock, and while I was there Mantu washed my feet. He said he was sorry that everyone had been a bit reticent in the early days but now they trust and care for me. It was just the thing I needed to hear at that point.

I really wanted to have a vision. Sadly I woke up here in my hammock having just slept through the whole thing. I have no idea if I dreamt or not, but I certainly don't remember anything. I'm gutted.

15 December. Wijint

This evening a baby jaguar cub was found in the area; he's blind in one eye so is never going to survive in the wild. He's a tiny little cub and he purrs away, hissing occasionally.

We have awful thoughts of him being sold downriver somewhere and put in a cage. We feel we should take him away so he can be looked after properly. But we don't know where. We've emailed a load of places to see if there is anywhere that could take him on. I'm very tempted to take him back to my home in Ibiza but I know I'll never get him there. Steve is humouring me but keeps gently pointing out the flaws in my plan!

16 December. San Lorenzo

This morning we left Wijint. I moved out of Mantu's place, leaving him and his family with affection – everything had worked out well, which was a huge relief as the Achuar's judgement of outsiders is coloured with an understandable mistrust. I'm glad that they feel suspicious of strangers like me, and I hope that this cynicism buys them more time in their difficult struggle with the corporations who want to extract natural resources from their land.

After the next twenty hours, which we'll spend vibrating to the noisy outboard motors of our tiny boats, we're heading back towards Lima for a much-needed Christmas break, and we'll resume our film in 2008.

BELOW: Bruce, Mantu and his family, with the shaman who conducted the ayahuasca ceremony

2008. 14 January. Andoas

PREVIOUS PAGE:
Filming began on the
Río Corrientes in the
New Year. Bruce and
the crew travelled
by boat to discover
the impact of the
oil industry on the
Achuar and their
environment

I spent most of Christmas in Colombia – the crew and I parted in Lima and most people returned to the UK for the festive period. In the New Year I returned to Lima to meet the crew again and it was great. We have one new team member, Pete – he's an experienced soundman and very funny, fifty years old and fit as a fiddle.

A couple of days ago we travelled to the familiar haunt of the prison block at San Lorenzo, where we picked up our Achuar friend Jorge, and then took two long boat journeys along the Marañón and Pastaza rivers to the petrol town of Andoas. The boats were the familiar small and noisy vessels and we drove into the rain hibernating like sardines under black plastic sheets. Hardly five star.

The main bar of Andoas is called *I'll Tell You Later*, and it appears to be a pretty drab place. Willow's been working very hard setting up a shoot in this area so we can film the impact of the petrol companies on the Achuar and the environment. Arriving here I can see why she has chosen Andoas as our base – it's hugely different from Wijint: there are concrete walkways and the neon glow of the oil plant lights up the night. There's an air of lethargy here; people are indifferent to our presence when we film, but there's also an underlying tension. We've heard rumours of a murder and a revenge plot and the sense of latent violence creates an uneasy undercurrent. Jorge had heard about the social changes to communities in the Corrientes area, but had never seen it at first hand. He was shocked and distraught by Andoas. His first impressions, like mine, are of unhappiness and depression.

15 January. Andoas

Today was desperately frustrating as our first vehicle had been lent elsewhere and torrential rain over mud roads meant various substitute vehicles failed to materialize. It's essential to the film that we get around the area to see the impact of the oil extraction and all of us are feeling the stress a bit, especially Steve, myself and Willow. We've come all this way and there is the potential that we will run out of time and not film any of the destruction of the environment. The rejuvenated mood we've all shared since our Christmas break has evaporated as we feel the film slipping through our fingers. I hate the time pressures of this trip.

16 January. Jose Olaya

Today we finally got a vehicle to take us to the village of Jose Olaya, where we picked up Guevara, an environmental monitor for his community. Working for an oil company is better paid than monitoring any impacts, but feelings against the oil companies run high and there are many monitors willing to investigate environmental damage. Guevara told us there'd been two spills recently: one seventeen days previously and another only a few days ago, which we were not permitted to see as it was within a fenced company area.

Our journey was stalled by a hill. Our driver had only done his off-road driving course the day before and the road was a mud slick. We ended up stuck all day.

Some very friendly guys from the oil company came and helped, but to no avail. It was good to get me interacting with these men on camera because it means we can show that the average oil worker is a normal person doing a job, who shouldn't be demonized. Finally at dusk a gorilla of a truck dragged us out of the ditch and we returned to Jose Olaya demoralized. Like yesterday, it's terribly frustrating. Everybody is paranoid that we might get stuck again on our one day left; but we're all desperate to see this environmental damage, it's the reason we've spent so much time, money and energy getting here. I know it will contain the shots that we need.

17 January. Jose Olaya

We discovered we could reach the older slick by dugout so we hopped on board first thing this morning, travelled upriver for two hours, and then walked through jungle.

We helped each other across logs on the trek and saw some small primates bouncing around but all the time there was the ominous sound of a tremendous hum and grind. We saw enormous generators, emerging from the jungle into an expanse of cleared ground, pipes everywhere and heat, steam and dust – thoroughly ugly and a huge contrast to the life of the forest.

The rain started to pour and we found the site of destruction. It had already been cleaned up massively, and there was a patch of completely bare earth – the foliage ripped out with large areas of dark tarry refuse and organic material. It was hideous. The downpour only added to the vision of apocalypse.

Oily petroleum was flooding into rivulets like black poison and we followed the stream on its way to the Río Corrientes, from which Guevara, his family and his neighbours drink, fish and wash.

We could have spent weeks uncovering other similar sites of devastation. Corrientes was one of the first areas explored for oil in the 1970s and the story is tragic. The Achuar were hardly consulted and the first thing they knew was that their land was suddenly crawling with strangers. First came the exploration, cutting tracts for miles through the forest and detonating explosives. Then the extraction started

with rigs and drilling platforms. All the labourers would hunt and log timber as they wished, competing with local people. The roads gave easy access to illegal loggers and poachers. Disease, poisoning, prostitution and community destruction is the price the Achuar have paid for having many billions of dollars beneath their ancestral lands.

It's not simple. Most of us use fossil fuels in nearly everything we do and every country has a right to use its natural resources if they don't threaten the lives of their citizens in the process. Many of the worst atrocities happened a long time ago now, and the government of Peru has recently instructed the oil company to cease some of its more damaging polluting practices. There are legal battles over compensation being fought as I write.

The Achuar here are a changed people and watching Jorge and Guevara interact is telling. Jorge is adamant that the Achuar of Wijint can never let this happen to them. He can see that the Achuar here in the Corrientes valley have electricity, outboard engines, some healthcare and schooling, but as Guevara unwaveringly puts it, 'We would give it all up to have our land back as it was.'

20 January. Iquitos

After Corrientes we went back on the boats to San Lorenzo, bidding farewell to Jorge before travelling on to Iquitos. We entered a port called Belen, which is a vibrant floating village that hosts a market selling the natural produce from the local Amazon.

There were so many boats moored we had to tie up and clamber across two or three other boats before we even got to dry land. We raced around the town on scooter chariots – motorbikes with a trailer, which carry three or four people and seem to be used all along the Amazon. I enjoyed tearing through the dust on the scooter chariots, meeting strangers in neighbouring chariots at traffic lights and visiting the colonial park that was built during the rubber boom.

We found a few bars overlooking Iquitos's swampy surrounds: we're at the confluence of the Marañón and the Ucayali, where the river is called the Amazon for the first time. We did some filming of the enormous river here. It's full of floating debris slowly revolving in giant whirlpools, and after three months we can finally say we're on the Amazon itself!

21 January. Near Iquitos

When I took ayahuasca before Christmas I was disappointed not to have a vision, but it's unusual to hallucinate taking the Achuar brew because, unlike many other cultures, the Achuar don't mix the ayahuasca vine with the other leaves that augment

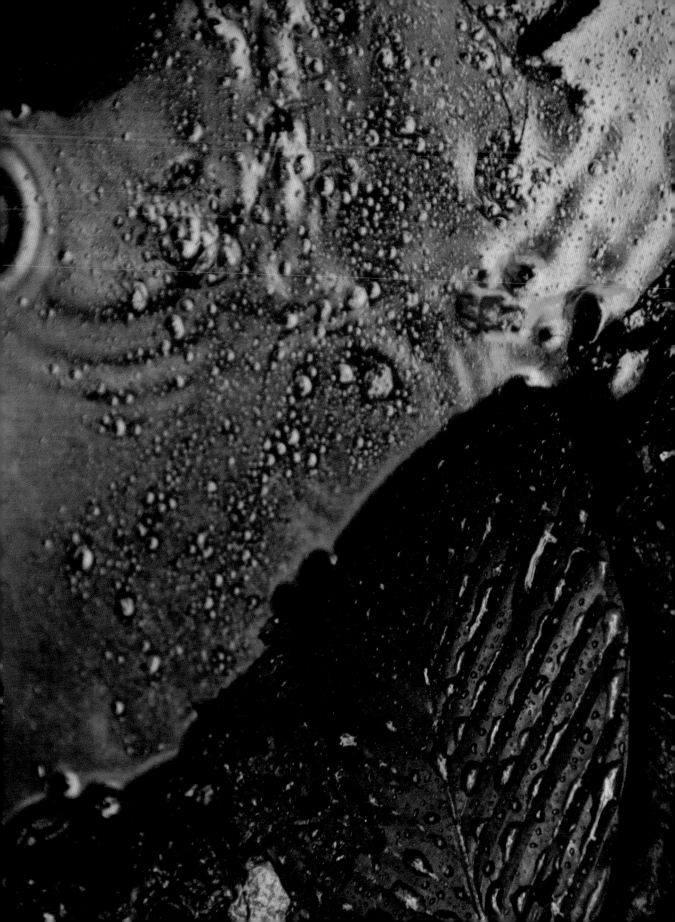

PREVIOUS PAGE:
The port of Belen in
Iquitos. The crew was
met here by armed
police who guarded
them on to shore.
The smell from the
water was detectable
streets away

its psychotropic effects. I wanted to experience the more potent version of ayahuasca because it's such an important ritual in the western Amazon. Leaving Iquitos this morning we went to Dios Ayahuasca Sanaciones, the ayahuasca centre run by Percy Lozano, a *curandero* (healer). Percy performs a similar role to an indigenous shaman but is not indigenous and prefers to describe himself as a catalyst for the ayahuasca.

Ayahuasca should not be taken carelessly and one reason for the presence of a shaman or healer is so that he can help out if it goes awry. I was initially concerned that Percy and I would find it difficult to communicate through the language barrier but once I met him my fears were allayed: he's relaxed and friendly and the retreat itself is perfect, in a jungle clearing with stilted wood pagodas around a brook.

This morning I continued with my diet of foods without salts or strong flavours, as is advisable before taking ayahuasca, and Percy showed us around his land. He gained his knowledge from his uncle, a trader who used to meet lots of indigenous peoples. In addition to an interest in commodities his uncle was a keen chef, so he was always getting cooking tips; as a result he picked up lots of indigenous knowledge about plants and became a bit of an *ayahuascero* (ayahuasca shaman or master) himself.

Percy's description of plants was similar to that of many indigenous peoples I've met: everything has a male or female aspect; a relationship to a particular animal; and a strong or weak spirit. Percy mixes the ayahuasca vine with two plants, chacrona (which contains the hallucinogen DMT) and an even more powerful leaf of the datura tree. I'm expecting a potent experience over the next couple of days.

22 January. Near Iquitos

In the brook this afternoon I shared a ceremonial bathing with the other people who have come to take ayahuasca. Percy had spent the day collecting various beautiful-smelling plants and we went down into the water and came up one at a time for Percy to pour flowery essences over our faces and bodies. Percy then blew tobacco about our heads and the tobacco smoke circled around us (the tobacco plant is considered to have a powerful spirit).

People come to do ayahuasca for a variety of reasons, sometimes for spiritual exploration but equally often because they're searching for therapy for problems such as childhood trauma or substance addiction. The ayahuasca ceremony is this evening and I expect it to be profound and traumatic.

ABOVE: The brook of the ayahusaca retreat in which participants take their ritual wash before the ceremony

23 January. Iquitos

It's the day after the ayahuasca experience. In the afternoon before I took the drug I saw a two-metre fer de lance – a pit viper renowned for its dangerous, territorial instinct – and my initial reaction, which I resisted, was to kill the snake. Snakes are powerful omens in ayahuasca dreams so I wondered what this encounter foretold.

The crew were going to film the build-up to the ceremony but as soon as Percy blew out the candle only Willow stayed to film with the small camera, so that we didn't perturb anyone with the huge camera and bright light. There was a big chair at a low table in the centre of the room. On the table there were essences, maracas and a Tibetan singing bowl. Facing the centre like the spokes of a wheel were single mattresses on the floor, each with a pillow, blanket and a bucket.

Percy entered dressed in his ritual costume – a bright silk jester's hat, some furry coronets atop it, and an Aertex tiger shirt over the top of a football shirt with some necklaces.

He blew tobacco smoke into a series of bottles and fastened each with its lid. Then he poured the ayahuasca into bowls and again poured tobacco smoke over the liquid. Everyone came up one at a time, as if they were at communion to take the sacrament, and stood in front of him. He handed them a bowl of ayahuasca with the smoke still in it and they drank. Most people instantly went to swill out their mouth with water because it tasted so acrid. The bowl went round the room and then came my turn. It was bitter and viscous, like treacle – very different from the watery brew I'd had with the Achuar.

I talked to the camera and the candles were blown out. We all lay back on to the mattresses and Percy started to sing. Not much happened but suddenly, after about an hour, I started seeing fireworks. I have a very black and white visual imagination – I never dream in colour – but suddenly there were vivid fireworks going off in my peripheral vision. Bring it on, I thought, but this cocky talk was to be my downfall.

I knew I needed to relax and let the plant get to work but at the same time the voice of my ego was talking against the visions and questioning what was happening. My ego, it seemed, was having a full-on scrap with Mother Ayahuasca. Unbelievable. The sheer audacity of it. Watching, as it were, from the sidelines, I was desperate for the plant to win and shut my ego up, but it was putting up a good fight. And that was the message: stop second-guessing everything. Stop thinking you always know best. Be in the moment. Listen to others. Truly listen and take in their message. Don't have an answer for everything just to prove you're cleverer. It was a strong message and delivered with extreme clarity. I asked for a second bowl of ayahuasca – to Percy's slight concern – just to try and give the plant a better chance at winning, but no matter what I did, my ego kept on making a bloody racket.

In one of my few visionary moments, I did have a conversation with the snake I'd met earlier: she asked me why I wanted to kill her and what she'd done wrong. She said that so long as I don't threaten her children or corner her we could get on fine, and told me my negative reaction to her was implanted in me by ignorant people living in fear.

Today I discussed my experiences with the others who are staying at the retreat. It's a really nice group from all over the world. Last night's thoughts and visions had been different for everyone, but all feel that their experience had been very beneficial. As for me, I feel humbled and promise to take on board some of the lessons I've learnt.

Filming in this area is now complete. I'm shocked and saddened by the devastation and contamination we've seen with the Achuar and reeling a little from my battle with ayahuasca; but it's time to leave Peru for Brazil, where our first week will coincide with the most profligate of Brazilian traditions – carnival!

'It's a strange and humbling thing to experience, even from mid-air – a completely isolated group of people in one of the last wildernesses of the world.'

CHAPTER 3
CONTACT

Bruce follows the Amazon into Brazil to live with remote tribal groups that have only recently been in contact with outsiders. On arrival he joins carnival, a festival first brought over by European settlers. Next he explores the Javari Reserve, the protected home of indigenous peoples who have lived in the forest since long before the coming of outsiders. Some of these tribes remain in isolation, avoiding all contact with the outside world. Non-indigenous people have highly restricted access to this reserve, which is the same size as Portugal.

Celebrated deep in the Amazon, carnival incorporates music from Africa, language from Europe and dance from Cuba. It was first celebrated in Brazil in 1840 as a Catholic masquerade ball but consequently absorbed the cultures of subsequent migrations to become quintessentially Brazilian.

These migrations to Brazil meant the indigenous tribes of the Amazon came into contact with people from overseas – an encounter that was all too often deadly. When Europeans first arrived in South America 500 years ago there were an estimated 5 to 7 million people living in Brazil. For the first few centuries of contact these people were often violently displaced, but in 1910 in Brazil the Indian Protection Service was established. Their motto was 'Die if you must but never kill', and they used expert Amazon explorers to seek out tribes with the aim of gently introducing them to the rest of Brazil. It was dangerous work but the explorers stayed true to their motto not to kill in violence.

However, bringing tribes into contact with new people also exposed them to new diseases and there are now only 300,000 indigenous people left in Brazil. The Matis are one of the surviving tribes, with a remaining 300 members living in the Javari Reserve. Matis people first appeared in 1976 on the banks of a river and contact with outsiders ensued from 1978, but with tragic consequences. They had no immunity to many common European infections such as flu, and diseases spread quickly through the population, leading to a huge demographic shock. In the 1980s the Matis claimed there were too few left healthy enough to bury their dead.

Other tribes had simply been part of a larger populace before the Europeans arrived, but became distinct groups once they had contact with outsiders. The

Marubo are a tribe born of such contact. During the rubber boom of the nineteenth century, a turbulent time of conflict and disease, the Marubo did not exist as one group. In the Javari headwaters, various indigenous groups fought each other and attempted to resist enslavement by rubber tappers. Fatalities spiralled until a powerful shaman united the people of the area into one strong group with the name Marubo. After the collapse of the rubber boom in 1910 the Marubo were isolated from outsiders until missionaries made contact in the 1960s.

The creation of the Javari Reserve forced outsiders and their infections to its boundary, and FUNAI (the modern version of the Indian Protection Service) stringently controls access to the forest, protecting the tribes and their forest dwelling. Loggers are not permitted within the reserve and work around its edge, providing hardwoods for an international and a Brazilian market. Despite these measures, lethal disease still affects tribes in the reserve, including the Matis and Marubo. There are a handful of clinics there, but no hospital. For Bruce and the crew, there is no choice but to evacuate anyone in their team who falls ill with malaria.

BELOW: Bruce wearing the hunting dress of the Marubo, a tribe still suffering from diseases brought in by outsiders

31 January. Leticia

The new crew flew out yesterday and landed during a powerful Amazonian storm. We've a new director, Rob, and with him are Leti, our assistant producer, and Laura, our researcher. Leti is a Brazilian who's been living in the UK for over a decade, and is a professional photographer and Amazonian expert; Laura has been a friend for years but this is our first time working together. They've joined Pete, Matt and me in the Colombian town of Leticia, right on the Brazilian border.

The electricity in Leticia has cut out and we spent our first evening telling stories by candlelight in our hotel while the sky emptied itself outside. Hopefully these malevolent-looking black clouds will clear for carnival.

1 February. Benjamin Constant

This morning we travelled by boat to the small border town of Benjamin Constant, arriving at the busy quayside in brilliant sunshine. There are lots of these small towns bordering Peru, Colombia and Brazil, each with their own mix of languages and nationalities. After barely getting used to Peruvian Spanish, I'm now trying to learn my first few sentences of Portuguese so I can understand some of what goes on in this bustling Brazilian town, which Leti thought would be the ideal place for us to join in Brazilian carnival.

In the town we were met by two guys, Vena and Tota; they wore matching black T-shirts with 'Soro', the name of their *bloco* (carnival community), emblazoned across the front in bright pink. They handed one to me and – now dressed appropriately – I jumped on the back of Vena's motorbike and we headed into the town, passing other taxis loaded with crates of beer, boys playing street football and girls parading their new outfits. The heat seemed to shimmer on the road and everywhere was excessively noisy.

Matt Norman was perched on the back of Tota's motorbike, filming backwards, and our travelling circus picked up a few grins and waves.

We arrived at the bungalow of Maria, a legendary dressmaker. We were there to kit ourselves out in drag for carnival.

I've worn my share of drag before – it's almost compulsory in the Royal Marines – and usually tried to look at least a *little* bit classy, but I could immediately see that this experience would involve cross-dressing of a particularly ugly fashion. The room was covered in fairly offensive fabrics: sequins, ribbons and chiffon – mainly in shades of virulent pink. As Vena scrutinized a sequinned brassiere, he asked who I thought was the more macho of the two of us. I told him it was him, then asked

how it was that such macho men would do this every year. Vena replied that you can only cross-dress if you are happy with your macho-ness, and that it's actually pretty macho.

And then I was handed a crimson thong.

2 February. Benjamin Constant

Today began with the cross-dressed football match, which was the best game of football I have ever played. I met the other members of the Soro *bloco* on the touchlines. The players were clad in leopard skin or frilled skirts and there was a lot of Lycra, stretched over hairy chests or pulled up to reveal paunchy beer guts. It was like an audition for Cinderella's sisters, and I took my place among the throng wearing a rather itchy pink number.

An on-hand make-up artist and a few crates of beer helped us to limber up and then we assembled on the pitch for kick-off. No one was sure who was on which side, although our defence included a huge chap dressed as a baby and sucking a dummy, and a goalkeeper barely three foot tall (which I thought was a stroke of brilliance).

The more ridiculous the play, the more the crowd cheered. The huge baby's star turn involved picking up the ball and running with it, and I had a pre-planned

hissy fit during a handbag scrap and was sent off for five minutes. Vena was referee, and would also get involved with the action, dribbling the ball around and using his position to yellow-card anyone who dared tackle him. The whole riotous experience lasted twenty minutes and nobody knew nor cared about the final score.

This evening was a far less comfortable experience. I had been entered into the *Queen of the Carnival Beauty Pageant*. I would never have volunteered for this frightful occasion but the production team had submitted my name months before. I was wearing a red minidress with matching pantomime lipstick – I looked atrocious, I felt nervous and I was dreading the catwalk. We turned up in the Samba-drome (a stadium) for the pageant just after eight, as a dusky sunset turned to night. *Brega* music was being played inhumanely loudly.

There was much hanging around, with the crew trying to keep up my spirits in a way that became more desperate as the hours passed. The other queens didn't arrive until about midnight and, once they had, we all ascended a rickety wooden platform behind the main stage to prepare for our turn on the boards. Safety in numbers meant it was more fun once the other guys were getting involved – the goalkeeper scurried about in knickers searching for his wig, and he eventually donned the windshield from Pete's mike, which lent him the appearance of a greying groovy diva.

I had been hoping to put in a classy turn on the catwalk – I'd been thinking understated glamour with a hint of risqué tease – but after watching a couple of guys strut their stuff it was apparent that a more shameless and silly performance was required. I hate performing like this but it was no occasion for half-measures. Once it came to my turn, I tottered out on my towering stilettos and gave a bit of a show: bending over to pick up my earring and waving my posterior before the judges, that sort of thing. Embarrassing.

4 February. Benjamin Constant

Yesterday was the masque ball, which aesthetically was fairly like Halloween. I was wearing a long robe with a devil's mask. The various *blocos* paraded around town and then into the Samba-drome, each group competing with the others to create the loudest sound they could.

The word 'Soro' means 'intravenous drip' in Portuguese, and the reason for the name became obvious: each of the guys in my *bloco*, including myself, had a plastic bag full of caipirinha cocktail with a tube from the bag directly into our mouths, so you constantly imbibed alcohol – the effect of which soon made it difficult for me to do any coherent pieces to camera. This dismayed Rob and amused everyone else.

All night, the tannoys blared out songs at full volume and everyone knew the lyrics, which meant there was a joyful and inclusive atmosphere with young and old people all singing along. It seemed like singing carols at home, but when I asked Leti for a translation she sang: 'My pants were clean, they were a present from my girlfriend, and I'll kill whoever used them as a dishcloth.' So, slightly different from 'Hark! the herald angels sing'.

The party continued until late last night, for all members of the family. Despite its roots, there was little evident debauchery. The word carnival itself is from the Latin *carne vale* and roughly translates as 'farewell to the flesh'. It first came to Brazil through the Portuguese Catholics, who celebrated the festival as a final indulgence before renouncing fleshy pleasures for Lent. The origins of the festival are thought to be even older, dating right back to Greek spring festivals honouring Dionysus, the god of wine, and then mixed with bacchanalian revelry in the Roman era, when slaves and masters would swap clothes once a year.

The Brazilian samba setting seems to reflect a lot of the external cultural influences that have made Brazil – from Europe, Africa and Cuba. In its own uniquely flamboyant way, Brazilian carnival seems to show the connection between Brazil and other cultures, both ancient and modern, around the world, although I didn't notice any representation of local indigenous people in the festival.

6 February. Benjamin Constant

Yesterday we discovered that the pilot we had booked to do aerial shots over the forest had crashed because he'd forgotten to put down the landing gear. No one was badly injured but the underbelly of the plane was ruined.

A lot of ringing around ensued, with Leti calmly translating several simultaneous conversations, and eventually we found a missionary plane called Wings of Mercy.

Wings of Mercy use the money from commercial flights to supply medical provisions to indigenous people, so we didn't mind shelling out the small fortune it cost to get the plane from Manaus, which is a five-hour flight away.

Once in the air we flew over the *Vale do Javari*, a vast reserve about the size of Portugal, which is a designated Indigenous Peoples Reserve. It's home to the Matis and Marubo tribes, who, along with the other tribes, number about 4,000 people living in the rainforest reserve. There are also at least five (and quite probably more) groups that avoid contact with outsiders. We flew over Aurelio, where we shall be spending time with the Matis; and then up to the headwaters, where the Marubo live.

Last year, people in one of the Marubo villages realized that manioc had disappeared from their fields, which troubled them. Months later a woman was working in her garden and she looked up to see a number of men standing silently in front of her; they were much darker than her, with black hair that hung right down their backs. She screamed for help and the men fled.

FUNAI, the Brazilian government's Indigenous Protection Service, was informed of the sighting. About six months ago Tota, one of the FUNAI representatives for the area, came across some huts on an aerial flight over the region, which he thought must have belonged to the uncontacted group, but he hadn't been able to take a GPS reference. Tota had agreed to come with us today to talk about the reserve, and we flew over a location that he thought might be near the uncontacted area. Unfortunately, the weather was closing in and we were very low on fuel. The pilot wanted to return and we were in no position to argue.

Suddenly, Marco, our Brazilian fixer, spotted a gathering of a few huts, minuscule in the endless sea of trees. I couldn't see any people, just huts in a small clearing near a brook. Tota confirmed that this was the same settlement he'd found and he noticed that their manioc field was a little larger, which is an indication that they are prospering.

From FUNAI's perspective this is a valuable sighting, but we had no idea what they would make of a plane above them, and we felt it was important not to hang around in case our presence felt threatening to them. So we left.

LEFT: The Wings of Mercy missionary plane. All profits are donated to supply medical provisions for indigenous people

BELOW: A gathering of huts belonging to an isolated forest group. Very little is known about the inhabitants, of which there are only two recorded sightings

The *Vale do Javari* has probably the largest concentration of isolated tribespeople in the world. Some may be completely new groups with unknown languages and cultures, while others have probably splintered from tribal groups and gone deeper into the forest, possibly to avoid the persecutions of the past. Previously FUNAI policy was to contact these people and let them know about the outside world, but the reality is that contact has been devastating for Indians. They've suffered death and disease; huge psychological and social traumas; and often the collapse of their culture. Now, because of bitter experience, the current FUNAI policy is to leave isolated groups alone.

It's a strange and humbling thing to experience, even from mid-air – a completely isolated group of people in one of the last wildernesses of the world.

7 February. Benjamin Constant

A huge surprise for us all today when Leti told us that she's just discovered she's pregnant – a significantly bigger surprise for Leti herself!

Everyone is delighted for her and we've all had somewhat heightened emotions since hearing the news. Leti's got to leave us to return to the UK and we'll miss her sorely, both as a friend and because she's done a vast amount of the preparatory work for all the Brazil phases of the trip.

9 February. FUNAI post

We're on the Javari and Itui rivers, travelling to film with the Matis, in a community that I filmed with in 2006 to make an episode of *Tribe*. It's strange to be returning, and I've been remembering old friends and experiences on the journey: being painted with a jaguar pattern by Tumi, my host; the constant banter amongst the guys in the longhouse; and Tumi's wilful five-year-old son coming to shake my hammock and wake me up.

I feel some trepidation on my return. The tribes have been suffering recently from catastrophic epidemics – particularly of malaria and also hepatitis.

As with my last visit, we need to stop here at the FUNAI post to show our medical documentation and prove we've been inoculated and are in good health.

It's possible that when I return to my old friends I'll find them living in fractured communities, suffering from illness and grief. I very much hope not, but I'm trying to prepare myself for a shock.

10 February. Beija Flor

We stopped here at the community of Beija Flor, which is the only other Matis village. We're leaving them gifts equal to those we'll give to the village of Aurelio during our filming trip, so that we don't create any economic imbalance between the neighbouring villages.

I have spent a couple of nights here before, and a few of the guys remembered me. It was good to see them. It was late when we arrived and, once in bed, I slept like a log.

11 February. Aurelio

Our boats arrived today at Aurelio, and, like the last time I came here, there was a bit of a crowd collecting when our boat pulled up – but this time there were few smiles.

When I climbed up the bank, almost everyone met me with the same words: 'We are dying.'

Forty years ago the Matis had no contact with outsiders. Last time I was here, Txema (pronounced 'Chema'), the chief, had told me that when the outsiders first arrived all the Matis had been shocked by their terrible stink. The Matis have got used to the smell of others since then but they haven't got used to their diseases: there were catastrophic epidemics in the eighties and, tragically, it's happening again.

On my last trip Txema's son had been sick and now I find out that he is dead.

Tumi, my former host, greeted me warmly. His son, Tumi junior, had grown up lots and seemed as cheeky and robust as ever. His daughter, however, was sick with hepatitis, and her own baby daughter had a fever that could be malaria.

Understandably people wanted us to film a meeting about the sickness immediately. They are very angry. During the meeting there was a subdued atmosphere. People seemed more perturbed by the film crew this time around – particularly by the boom pole and huge furry mike.

This evening we showed them the *Tribe* film we had made here. When we had arrived last time they were initially reluctant about us filming – saying that previously they'd had a bad deal from outsiders. Eventually we had won their trust and we'd promised to make a film that portrayed them as accurately as we could. I was interested to see their reaction.

Everyone made a big fuss about the light from the projector and chattered excitedly throughout the film. They asked constantly about the actions on screen, comments like: 'Where are we going now?'; 'That's not a good place for hunting, we won't find any monkey there'; 'Are we going to do the frog poison again to him?'; 'He's too weak to manage it'; 'What's he doing now?'; 'We've made him really ill'; 'No, he just needs to shit.'

At the end everyone seemed pleased, which was a real relief, because this is

the most important audience the film has ever had. I told them that we would also allow them to speak on camera about the things they want to talk about, just like we did that time. But I went to bed wondering, in the background of that film, which people were no longer here, and how it was for my friends to see their faces again on screen. I feel concerned for their difficulties and I'm wondering how our film can help and what else can be done.

12 February. Aurelio

This morning I moved into Tumi's house – taking the same hammock that I had two years ago. My first task was to go with Tupa, his wife, to collect manioc. As we collected the plant Tupa said, 'We may be dying, but we still have to live,' and gave me a broad, welcoming smile.

In the afternoon we went to the health clinic, which is run by a Brazilian nurse called Giliana. Giliana said she is the only trained clinician in this huge area, albeit with a few assistants. There is a radio in the clinic and while I was there she was on it repeatedly, trying to respond to emergencies over the air. She can't get to places because her fuel and boat resources are so restricted. She's determined and inspirational but there is a limit to what can be done by one nurse with a radio.

It seems as if there have been a lot more resources promised compared to what is actually coming through to people in the area. I don't know enough to have a reliable judgement but there have been numerous accusations of corruption somewhere along the chain of delivery. It angers me to think of some greedy person getting rich with money intended for the communities that are left to suffer.

ABOVE: Bruce with women and children in the Matis village of Aurelio. Village life continues despite catastrophic epidemics, as Tupa (second left) says, 'we may be dying but we still have to live'

13 February. Aurelio

RIGHT: Visiting Aurelio was not without its pleasures, such as the attention of this woolly monkey, but the village was subdued and many Matis were anxious about their future

PREVIOUS PAGE: Tumi with three of his children. The family hosted Bruce in 2006 and 2008, during this time Tumi feels his community has become increasingly dependent on outside aid

This morning started in the traditional Matis way – huddling together in the door of Tumi's longhouse while the air gets warmer and the sun rises higher. Then I got to work chopping wood before setting off to collect peach palm fruit.

Later I joined Tumi senior showing Tumi junior how to make arrows. This seems to be a rare exchange, as most of the younger Matis prefer to hang out or play football. Tumi explained that very few seem interested in learning the skills of their fathers and there appears to be the growth of a culture of dependency on gifts and aid received from outside agencies and visitors. Our presence here would contribute to this.

Tumi expressed sadness at what he saw as the inevitable loss of community independence that was resulting from external influences and the desire for more material goods. But he agreed that it was patronizing to stop change once people knew about other ways of life. Town is not far away and although outsiders are restricted from coming in by FUNAI, the Matis can leave whenever they want. Most had been to town and many to the big cities.

The movement of Matis also brings more infections to the community at Aurelio. Although outsiders undoubtedly brought the first wave of disease to the Matis, the current hepatitis epidemic could have been caused by sexual encounters between Matis and townspeople. The infections come back to the villages and spread further, and then people get sick and can't access the clinics.

Eating in the longhouse was just as it had been two years ago, with the same joviality and communal atmosphere. But the men there echoed what Tumi said: they wanted western medicine; they didn't want to struggle with illness any more.

Most of the Matis shamans were killed in the first epidemic of illness in the eighties, and their medicinal knowledge died with them. The Matis here didn't want shamans, they wanted outsiders to bring drugs and treatments.

14 February. Vida Nova

We left Aurelio today. Before leaving I went to bid my farewell to Txema. He was with his daughter, who was still very sick, and not getting any treatment. I can tell that he is still grieving and angry about the death of his son, and feeling anxious about his daughter.

When I departed the village came to say goodbye – they told me they were sorry they had been downhearted, but they are sad and anxious. The Matis feel it is wrong to be too joyful in a time of death, so some had taken out their facial decorations as a sign of respect, which contributed to the subdued and sober atmosphere.

Tumi told me that although I was not one of them, I was a friend, and people surrounded me, placing necklaces on me and tying a capybara bone under my nose.

It was an emotional goodbye because I feel like our relationship is different after this second meeting, as if it has more depth and longevity. It's not like I've just spent a whirlwind visit with them. I've seen my friends looking older, their children grown up, and tragically, I've seen their suffering.

15 February. Vida Nova

Yesterday evening Matt and I, now veterans of small-boat travel, prepared our nests for the eighteen-hour journey to the Marubo communities upstream, each following our own practised individual system of bags and therma-rests, and eventually we set off.

At dusk, travelling upstream, I gained an idea of the extreme remoteness of this area. It's hard in the jungle to get a sense of space – as you literally can't see the wood for the trees – but last night I could feel the forest stretching around me for hundreds of miles. It was a very peaceful moment.

In contrast, today has been a rather stressful day of boat problems. We've been beset by a combination of engine difficulties and merciless sandflies. The steering mechanism broke this morning, so we transferred into dugout canoes. Then the engines cut out on these, and our captain used his sandals to paddle, and we all joined in with our own shoes until we got to the next village.

Eventually, after a great deal of tinkering with metal and swearing in Portuguese, we arrived in Vida Nova to meet people from all the communities in the area, and to give them some gifts – largely fuel – and explain to them why we can only film in one location. Everyone understood our explanation, so fortunately we haven't offended any of the communities with whom we're not going to film, and neither have we unbalanced relationships between villages.

16 February. Paraná

This morning at the missionary outpost, we awoke to find that Elena, the anthropologist who is travelling with us during the Marubo phase of the trip, was feverish and shivery. There's a medical clinic at the outpost so we tested her immediately for malaria, which she had – so we needed to evacuate her. The rest of us were also all tested and fortunately screened negative.

We left her waiting for her plane at the outpost and travelled in bright morning sunshine to the Marubo village of Paraná, which stands proudly on a hill at the headwaters of the village. Robson met me on the bank – he's a Marubo shaman,

LEFT: Travelling upstream toward the Javari headwaters, an extremely remote area of the westernmost Brazilian jungle

only twenty-seven, and seemed reserved on first meeting, but he is a renowned healer throughout the Javari region and his presence in this village is one of the reasons we chose to film here. He hugged me and took me into the huge palm-roofed longhouse in the centre of the village.

Inside the longhouse it was pitch dark, and I could see nothing as my eyes adjusted from the dazzling sunshine outside. To my huge surprise I felt strong hands grasp my thighs and I was hoisted into the air, on to the shoulders of one of the Marubo men. He ran up and down the length of the house about three or four times, holding me aloft. Around me I could hear cheering and whooping and soon dark outlines came into view and I could see that the house was full, with people lined up along the sides.

Once this unusual welcome was over, we were settling into a meeting when news came that Marco, our fixer, felt unwell too. He's had malaria before and his symptoms were familiar to him. We rushed to get him back on the boat to Vida Nova, so that he could hopefully meet the same plane that is coming to pick up Elena. We've now lost three members of the team, and are down to only one Portuguese speaker, Philippe, who we found to come in place of Leti.

Despite all the action it was still only 9 a.m. by this point and the Marubo had an entire day of ceremonies planned for us. It began in the longhouse, where they performed a series of very simple dances. The significance of each was explained by the chief of the village and Robson: 'This is the song that tells how we were formed'; 'This is the song told to us by a mystic bird that only the shaman can see'; 'This is the song about the making of the longhouse.'

Each of the many songs seemed to be a real confirmation of Marubo identity. They are sung in a special vocabulary reserved for mythic and curing chants, but because they are not words used in everyday Marubo a lot of people, it seemed, had forgotten the words and needed to copy others.

RIGHT: The longhouse is the central location of Marubo communal life, providing the setting for meals, sleep, discussions and ritual

17 February. Paraná

I'm staying here in the longhouse – my hammock is near the men's discussion area and today I went out hunting with some of the villagers. We shot a macaw and ate it.

Once evening came I watched Robson, the shaman, performing a cure for the chief's son, who has malaria. He's about sixteen and he's very sick. Earlier today I'd seen him roll over from his hammock and vomit a huge intestinal worm – about the length of my arm. Robson's shamanic speciality is to conduct the souls of the dead through the path to their final destination, making him the most powerful shaman of the Marubo, but fortunately this was a purely curative ceremony. I hope it works.

18 February. Paraná

The morning started with a health meeting, which the Marubo, just like the Matis, were very keen that we film. They are suffering the same diseases, including TB and hepatitis, and there are at least ten known cases of malaria in the village right now, including that of the chief's son.

Next, they had another ceremony planned. Despite our requests that we film their normal day-to-day lives, the Marubo are insistent that the way to experience their culture is through participating in their rituals. It seems we have no choice.

Today's ritual begins with us digging at the roots of trees for the tucandeira ant – a stinging ant that is used to help pass on the shaman's wisdom to the Marubo in order to make them stronger and more knowledgeable about their songs. I realize that at some point one of these is going to sting me, which alarms me, as I'm allergic to wasps and hornets. It's possible that this sting could send me into anaphylactic shock so I dose up on antihistamines in preparation. Everyone deposits their ants into the bowl I am carrying, which I hold at arm's length.

Once we return we each make a decorated wooden peg that we use to clasp our ant at the thorax, leaving its huge venomous abdomen sticking out of the rear. Prior to this we've all painted red dots on our skin to mark where we want the ants to sting – some people have, rather alarmingly, gone for exceptionally painful places such as the end of the nose or corner of the eye. Luckily I get no say in the matter, and as a first-timer, I've ended up with a dot in the fold of each arm.

After an hour of song and dance, the chief rubs the ant's arse on each dot until I feel the sharp pain of the sting. Around me there are a lot of squeals as my companions are stung all over their faces and bodies. Luckily, a serious reaction has been avoided, but my whole arm has gone red and the skin around the injection points has risen in large welts. Different!

19 February. Paraná

My forearms are still red and painful to touch. As is the Marubo way, we begin the day again with a ceremony, this time cutting a tree from the opposite bank and carving it into a drum. The performance of the ceremony lasts the entire day.

The Marubo insistence on ceremony is slightly different to my experience of ritual with other tribes. Of course, this could be an anomalous experience because they're performing for our visit, but to me there seems to be an element of coercion in these ceremonies that I find very interesting.

As a single tribe, the Marubo didn't exist until the early twentieth century, when a shaman called João Tuxaua congregated a cluster of peoples with different

LEFT: The Marubo of Paraná were friendly and welcoming but there were at least ten known cases of malaria in the village, with both the young and old suffering from the illness

BELOW: Pouring over pictures in *Tribe*, the Marubo see images of other forest peoples around the world, such as this picture of the Kombai of West Papua, Indonesia

languages. This coincided with the end of the rubber boom – a turbulent time when people needed unity in numbers to deal with oppression, slavery and war. João Tuxaua is thought to have shaped the whole ethos of Marubo culture, unifying the myth songs and cosmology of the groups into one complex system. Perhaps he also created new ceremonies, which drew on the historical cultures of the people but with the purpose of reinforcing their new collective identity.

Everything seems pretty regimented here, right down to the haircuts. The result is unity, which, combined with extreme isolation, has had the desired effect of making the culture proud and strong – people here seem very happy being Marubo and are lovely to me and to each other. But I couldn't help myself from asking a question during an interview with the schoolteacher, which almost sent Rob into shock. I wanted to know whether the teacher thought the Marubo were a superior culture to other tribal groups. His answer was yes. It makes me wonder how they will interact with their neighbours when the time comes and it was a fascinating contrast to the Matis, who, according to Tumi, are losing some elements of their grandparents' culture.

20 February. Paraná

RIGHT: Gathering plants in preparation for a ceremony. The Marubo's celebration of their strong sense of identity was apparent in many of the ceremonies Bruce experienced

Today began with the ceremony of the log drum. The men carried the enormous log back to the longhouse while the women ran up and chose a man to tickle. We needed to continue carrying the log and show our strength despite the distraction of the fingers in our ribs. This was a fun, tender ritual – even very young girls were coached in this gently flirtatious technique by their grandmothers.

Then in the afternoon Matt Norman, who is the only crew member who has been with me right since the source of the Amazon, began to feel ill. We got Matt tested for malaria in the rudimentary village clinic, and it came up positive, so we all went immediately into evacuation mode – having become experts at it now.

Two hours later a plane took him away. The incongruity of an evacuation from a community in epidemic did not escape those of us left behind. Luckily the Marubo were very understanding and shared our concern and desire for Matt's speedy transit to hospital. It has been one of the few times in my career that my life and the lives of my gracious hosts have been brought into such deadly, uncomfortable contrast.

21 February. Rio Itui

It's morning. I'm soaking wet and I've been awake for about thirty hours. We've just left the Marubo and we're on the boat heading to a missionary post.

We stayed up all night with the Marubo; it was hard work because we were knackered, but we needed to do so to show our gratitude to our lovely hosts. We all enjoyed the usual songs and dances. Towards the end of the evening Robson performed a shamanistic ritual in which he sucked the illness from a small baby and showed us the residue in his mouth – brown and green solids. I don't know what it was but everyone was in awe at his abilities. He's an amazing man and he has an incredibly important and difficult job to do in his community.

As we were leaving there was a mud fight going on between a few of the young lads, and they were casting the odd look in my direction with a noticeable glint in their eyes – so I decided I'd join in on my own terms by somersaulting into the river.

Loads of people lined up on the bank to wave goodbye. It was good. I'm going to try to sleep on the boat for a couple of hours before we reach the missionary station.

22 February. Tabatinga

Yesterday we had breakfast with a missionary couple at the tiny village of Vida Nova. Cheryl and Paul are an American couple in their sixties and they've been working as missionaries with the Marubo for the last thirty years. They've created their own lonely patch of the Midwest right here in the jungle – complete with a vegetable garden, a satellite connection and homemade 'jelly'.

They were both very gracious. Much of their work involves learning Marubo and translating the Gospels into Marubo with the local community. In fact, as a schoolchild, Robson lived in this village and he was the star at Gospel translation. Their education has given the Marubo the ability to engage with the rest of the world, and Robson is a good example of this – he can interact well with outsiders and when he was younger was expecting to go to university. Illness prevented him and during his treatment by a shaman he felt he began to understand the visions and dreams he had experienced since childhood and trained as a shaman himself; so the Christian education he had received did nothing to dampen his Marubo identity. Cheryl admitted freely that they had converted very few people to Christianity.

The mission doesn't offer healthcare any more, as that is the legal responsibility of FUNASA (a government agency), but people in the village informed us that over the years the missionaries have saved many lives with their medicines.

Ultimately, they're here to save souls, and they might not be here for much longer. Since the Javari Reserve was established there have been more and more calls to remove missionary presence from the area, because they're seen as a threat to the integrity of the tribes.

In my experience, each mission and each missionary need to be judged on their own merits. Some do wonderful things, and some certainly don't. But the truth is that often missionaries are the only people with the desire, the faith and the infrastructure to try to help the isolated tribespeoples of the world. They may have a disruptive second agenda but their presence often acts as a buffer to those who just want to exploit tribes and their land.

After leaving them we travelled through the day and the night to come back to Tabatinga, where we've got a couple of days off and a chance to feel washed and clean for the first time in weeks.

26 February. Rio Javari

We're staying in a tiny village near a viewing platform over the forest. We should have been going to stay at a logging camp today but our boat driver was pissed so we've gone up a platform to film the sun dip under the canopy. A fantastic view.

27 February. Logging camp, Rio Quixito

We've slung our hammocks up under the loggers' roof. Raimundo, the boss, greeted us as we arrived. He's a warm and welcoming man who has worked in the forest all his life. He can neither read nor write but he can survive in the forest.

PREVIOUS PAGE: Life
at a logging camp is
tough and physical.
Timber needs to be
transported across
large distances
and the loggers
at the edge of the
Javari Reserve take
full advantage of
floodwaters to help
them move chopped
up trunks

As we were interviewing him another guy, Boto, arrived with a woolly monkey on his back and proceeded to butcher the animal. Boto is a seriously cool hardman, with tattoos and a mighty jaw, and I instantly warmed to him.

These guys are expert hunters and they are almost completely self-sufficient. They spend about eight months of the year working, but go to the city in the dry season. They don't practise clear felling; instead they selectively fell the larger trees, chop them into four-metre sections and then roll them to the river in order to raft them into town.

This afternoon we took advantage of the rain to float the logs down a flooded stream to the river. It was wet and getting dark and we needed to run over the logs to make the most of the high water, and it took all my agility so that the logs didn't close in and crush my legs.

Now we're in the camp eating woolly monkey. It's a very male, very tough environment – the guys live in the outdoors and work physically hard all day. There are never any women here and already they've shared a lot of crass visual jokes about sexual frustration in the jungle.

28 February. Logging camp, Rio Quixito

Today I attempted to fell a tree. First these guys chopped down a few whopping specimens with a chainsaw. They handled the saw with ease, wearing only shorts and wellies (or even flip-flops) and without any safety gear at all.

Then it was my turn. I started to saw this huge tree, got halfway through, but during a short demonstration of what to do next, one of the loggers broke the chainsaw. Lucky it hadn't been me, because it is their only one in working condition. I asked Raimundo what a logger would do without a chainsaw. He looked at me as if I were a fool and said, deadpan, 'We've got axes, haven't we?' I felt stupid because for the majority of his life, that's exactly how he'd worked.

While the guys tried to fix the chainsaw Raimundo told me that he'd never come across any indigenous peoples, and he feels they've been given far too much land. Since the creation of the indigenous reserve, logging is restricted to the edge of the forest, although this is difficult to police. As a result there is a fair bit of resentment towards the reserve – which I was picking up from Raimundo.

1 March. Tabatinga

We said a farewell to Raimundo and his loggers, heading off downriver back to Tabatinga. I'm really glad to have met him and his team and, unexpectedly, I've

not enjoyed living with a community so much since I left Rodolfo in the Andes. The loggers have very few possessions but their warmth and hospitality has been extraordinary. Had I not visited them it would be easy to follow popular opinion and demonize such people, but nothing in the Amazon is that simple.

There are arguments that selective logging can be sustainable and should be allowed to continue throughout the Amazon, but I've learned from my time living with tribal groups like the Penan that, from their perspective, there is no such thing as logging in a sustainable way. To them, all such extraction has devastating effects on ecosystems. Added to that, selective logging could bring isolated tribes into contact with outsiders, as loggers need to encroach further into the forest to find the right trees. And that contact, of course, results in the terrible diseases that I've seen with the Marubo and with my friends the Matis.

The sad truth, which I'm discovering on my journey, is that so long as consumers continue to buy hardwoods while being ignorant of the destruction it's causing then the problem will persist.

Kind-hearted Raimundo is not to blame – he has no alternative offered to him by any government or agency. All he knows is that he enjoys the logging lifestyle and even though his family want him to retire to town, he told me that he would never go. The forest from which he waved goodbye to us this morning is his home too, and he wants to spend the rest of his life in the place that he loves.

ABOVE: Bruce attempts to fell a tree using a faulty chainsaw. When mechanized tools break, the loggers resort to axes to complete their work

'The water was dark and silent, and we swept our torch across the surface to reflect the red eyes of the caiman.'

CHAPTER 4
CONSERVATION

The next stop on Bruce's adventure is to take him into the heart of the wild Amazon, to the flooded forest of Amazonas State. This teeming ecosystem is home to species such as the pink river dolphin, the enormous black caiman, and the pirarucu – the largest scaled freshwater fish in the world. But the Amazon Basin also supports a human population of 20 million, 94 per cent of which live in a rural environment and are dependent on their surrounding natural resources. With so many people needing to make a living from the Amazon, the survival of its unique species is increasingly under threat.

Until the arrival of the Europeans in the sixteenth century, the indigenous people already there were living sustainably. The hunting, gathering and small-scale agriculture they practised was done in such a way as to maintain the Amazon's biodiversity, a result of centuries' worth of experimentation and knowledge of the area's ecological realities.

A huge wave of population arrived during the rubber boom – the cruel and oppressive industry initiated in 1850 when Europeans discovered the industrial potential of the *Hevea brasiliensis* tree. In order to tap rubber from the trees people were brought to the Amazon from all over Brazil, slaves arrived from Africa, and many of the indigenous peoples were subjugated. The industry in Amazonas prospered until new

Malayan plantations began to dominate the global rubber market. Amazonas' industry spiralled into decline, and those who hadn't died were left to fend for themselves.

Many of this remaining population live alongside the rivers and lakes of Amazonas and they have become known as *ribeirinhos*, literally 'river people'. They fish, hunt and grow manioc – the starchy tuber eaten across the Amazon Basin. *Ribeirinhos* are one of the many populations dependent upon the Amazon for food and trade, but in the last few decades the species upon which their livelihood depends have become endangered.

On the confluence of the rivers Japurá and Solimões, scientists and *ribeirinho* communities have worked together to try to create a solution to this problem. Mamirauá Reserve, the first Sustainable Development Reserve in Brazil, is an area of 11,000 square kilometres of flooded forest. It connects with two other reserves in a combined protected area larger than Costa Rica. *Ribeirinho* communities are vital in the reserve, both in maintaining the sustainable use of resources and by policing the remote areas of the reserve's 800 lakes.

Using a combination of science and economics, the reserve's rare species, such as the gigantic pirarucu, have increased exponentially over the last decade. The ecosystem is flourishing, and the resulting natural wealth provides financial benefit for those local communities permitted to sell the fish. For a village to become involved with these management programmes its inhabitants must prove they are monitoring their fish stocks and only taking sustainable amounts.

Bruce and the crew visit two communities in Mamirauá; one village is heavily involved in the reserve's conservation programmes but the other is still working to meet the necessary criteria. Here, at the ecological frontline, Bruce is to investigate what sustainable conservation means for local people and for the incredible wildlife of the Amazon.

ABOVE: Sunset over the flooded forest of Mamirauá – the first Sustainable Development Reserve created in Brazil

8 March. On board the *Fenix*

It's a humid night and I'm swinging in my hammock on the top deck of an Amazon passenger ferry. There are about 200 people on the boat, spread over three decks, and when I sit up I look along rows of other brightly coloured hammocks, their occupants all swaying to the movement of the boat, dozing and chatting. A few couples are sharing and a mother is sleeping with her baby against her chest. Everywhere is covered in bags and from the deck above a music system pumps Brazilian *forró* music.

Today was the first day of filming for Film 4, and with a new crew once again, we're travelling eastwards along the Amazon, away from the borders of Peru and Colombia. Leading us is Matt Brandon, returning after a complete recovery from his near-fatal brain infection back in November. It's great to see him so healthy after that traumatic experience in Peru.

The river is a favoured smuggling route for cocaine, so about an hour ago, when the river narrowed, there was a scheduled police raid. The narco-cops came on board without dogs and, instead, they went through everyone's bags by hand. They looked everywhere with a cynical eye: prising open brand new boxes of electrical goods, CD players and even splitting open a few banana skins to check inside.

On the boat in front, the police found a briefcase belonging to a man, which they thought was suspiciously heavy. They cut through the silk lining of the case and beneath it found about five kilograms of cocaine. On our boat, another couple of kilograms were found secreted in the lining of a case carried by a guy a few hammocks away from me. It's possible to make a lot of money trafficking cocaine, and the temptation to make years' worth of salary in a few days can be too much to resist for some. But the risks are high: for each kilogram it is possible to get between five and fifteen years in a Brazilian prison.

Those men that had been found in possession of the drug were handcuffed and taken to a floating office on the riverbank, which was dimly lit by a single blue light surrounded by insects. The men were all in their twenties and showed no emotion as the officers casually chatted about jail sentences.

We embarked on our boat once again, and as I got back into my hammock it struck me how in just one moment life had completely changed for those guys: they'd gone from swinging in their hammocks to the accompaniment of music, to sitting handcuffed in a dingy riverside cell, facing bleak prospects. They are unlikely to have ever tried the drug that changed their lives.

LEFT: Passengers swing in hammocks on the deck of the *Fenix*, one of the many passenger ferries operating along the Amazon

PREVIOUS PAGE: Brightly dyed chicks on sale in the border town of Tabatinga, which lies on the banks of a known cocaine smuggling route

9 March. On board the *Fenix*

This is my first time taking public transport on this trip and it's been a good opportunity for me to chat to other travellers along the river. At mealtimes everyone goes to the galley, queues up and then sits down together for dishes of spaghetti, fish, rice and beans.

I've met a number of interesting passengers, including John, an electrician from Hull; Pedro, a professional footballer who had the dubious pleasure of seeing me in drag in the Queen of the Carnival beauty pageant; as well as many others, including a man carrying a huge beetle. Many people are taking a break from their work in the city to visit their home villages but some are traders and a few are travellers like me. Shirley is a traveller from China (she has a proper Chinese name that she says is far too difficult for me to pronounce), who has entertained us with innumerable stories of her frustrating and almost farcical visa problems. Unperturbed by suspicious border officials who expect her to be an illegal immigrant, she is journeying throughout South America, with only one bag the size of a school knapsack. My journey, with half a ton of kit in thirty bags, could hardly be more different and I feel a little ashamed.

10 March. On board the *Spectrum*

The day started with collisions between our ferry and two separate riverside villages. During the second accident we completely sank a smaller craft that had been moored next to the space we were aiming for. It wasn't, therefore, with too much regret that we all said goodbye to the *Fenix* and cross-decked on to the *Spectrum*. This is a small private boat that will be our filming base for this phase of the trip. It has a crew of five, and is proudly captained. It's beautifully clean – not a cockroach in sight. For us, individual cabins, showers, flushing toilets, warm water and proper electric lights feel like unparalleled luxury. I could hardly bring myself to catch Shirley's eye as I waved the *Fenix* goodbye.

We're travelling to Mamirauá Reserve, the first Sustainable Development Reserve created in Brazil. It's different from many Biological Reserves because rather than excluding local people from the area as is often the case, it promotes sustainable community living in the natural environment. We've just dropped anchor by the village of Jarauá. It's a very dark night and I can just make out the calls of howler monkeys above the aggressive din of the boat's generator.

Mamirauá Reserve protects an area of flooded forest and over 800 lakes, and involves the communities in the preservation of key species. We're here to experience the conservation of the Amazon in action.

11 March. Jarauá

We disembarked this morning by the stilted houses of Jarauá, strategically located at the entrance to the interlinked lakes of the Mamiraúá Reserve. In the dry season this channel is just a trickle of water, but this is impossible to believe now as the river is bursting with floodwater that has come downriver from the soil-rich slopes of the Andes. The river rises about fifteen metres during the six months of annual flooding. The flood not only joins together all the lakes of the reserve but covers all the surrounding forest too. These flooded forests, called *várzea*, line both sides of the Amazon all the way down to the coast, to a width of tens of kilometres.

First I met Dona Lourdes, the president of the community, in her stilted hut. The people here are known as *ribeirinhos*, literally 'river people', but they are also called *coboclos*, which is a common term used to describe all Brazilians who are mixed race – the descendants mostly of indigenous peoples, black slaves and Europeans. There are no direct descendants of the original tribal groups of the Amazon who inhabited the banks of this mighty river when it was first explored in 1500. Although it was reported that their huge villages could rival the civilizations of the Incas and Aztecs, all that now remains of these indigenous tribes are faint memories. In fact, most of the inhabitants of this area are descendants of the thousands brought here to work on rubber plantations.

On the sides of Dona Lourdes' hut is a watermark about a metre up, and she explained that in unusually wet seasons the water rises to flood the houses and everyone needs to climb in and out of windows. Dona Lourdes oversees another four villages in addition to Jarauá and she's also the mother of Jorge Tapioca, a legendary fisherman, who has been sent by the institution around South America explaining how he and his community manage their fish stocks.

Like Dona Lourdes, most of the village live in these huts, which are well equipped, with chairs and televisions and corrugated-metal roofs. As I spoke with her, rain drummed upon the roof and soaked somebody's washing that was strung up from the hut opposite. Dona Lourdes explained that there is a good relationship between the community and the scientific institute, with both groups exchanging ideas and learning from each other in order to find the best way of managing the species of the area.

This evening I spoke with other people from the community. Everyone sat around the edges of a hall while a russet dog lay sprawled in the middle of the room. I described my journey and explained that I wanted to learn about their way of life. Because they are at the entrance of the reserve, the community is quite used to the presence of visitors from outside – normally scientific researchers or journalists – and they welcomed us wholeheartedly.

12 March. Jarauá

Today I had my first experience of fishing in the flooded forest. Last night at the meeting I met Jorge Tapioca, the master fisher and son of Dona Lourdes. I've sat nearly all day in his dugout canoe, gliding through the water as 'Tapioca' (his nickname) propels the boat using just one paddle in a continuous figure-of-eight motion, so as not to splash and disturb the water.

It was ethereal in the forest, bright green woodland with a lake in place of a forest floor. The water was so still that it reflected each one of the trunks and saplings, and around us were the ghostly sounds of howler monkeys and the screeches of calling birds. White egrets flew low across the lake and light fell through the trees on to lily ponds. I spotted a sloth, completely still in the top branches of a tree above me.

We dropped our nets down by the side of the canoe. Tapioca says that if he leaves the nets for too long then the caiman and piranhas tear them to shreds, so we pulled them up almost instantly, and we'd already caught three fish.

13 March. Jarauá

Manuel, who like Dona Lourdes is also a leader in this community, showed me how he peels and washes the manioc, a common staple food of this area. First the root is peeled and then kept submerged in water for a few days in a canoe at the side of the lake. Once softened, the tubers are mashed and drained of their toxic cyanide by squeezing. Next the pulp is sieved and toasted on a huge griddle. A canoe paddle is used to stir and throw the tapioca up in the air so it all gets evenly cooked. The end product, called farina, is crunchy and granular, and is served with almost every meal.

While we were peeling the root this morning, Manuel explained that since the fishermen have followed the reserve's management plan, the fish numbers have doubled, tripled, and then quadrupled over the years. Managing fish stocks and selling them legally has meant that the ability of families in the village to eat and earn money has increased exponentially. But the early days were not easy. Nobody believed the biologists at first, and having a total embargo on fishing profitable species was very difficult for everyone. He believed his community was lucky to live in an area of such abundance, and he thought that the reserve and its programmes have been nothing but a blessing, partly due to the foresight of Dona Lourdes' late

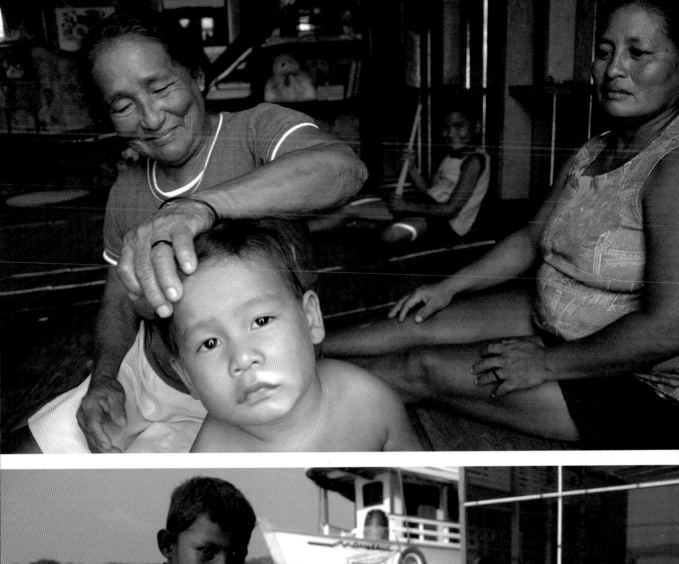

husband, who had headed the community at the time. Manuel described him as a visionary leader who could see the long-term benefits of the plan; he said that this prescience is missing in many of the communities of the area, who are fixed on making quick cash now, regardless of the future.

14 March. Jarauá

Today we went out with Tapioca to catch the largest scaled freshwater fish in the world. The pirarucu (*Arapaima gigas*) can reach 400 kilograms in weight – six times heavier than me! Its common name comes from the local indigenous language: *pirá* means 'fish' and *urucú* means 'red tail', referring to the deep red colouring around its scales. The fish is a flagship species for the reserve: in 1996 it was placed on the endangered list because numbers had fallen so low due to overfishing, but the scientists and the communities worked in partnership to manage the fish stocks and, as a result, they've recovered over the last decade. The pirarucu is so huge that one fish can either feed a whole village or command a good price in the markets of Manaus. The community have never even taken their full quota of the fish because they remember the old days of scarcity.

It's a giant catfish with a wide mouth and, unusually, it gulps air from the surface as well as using its gills underwater. Although it can survive for a miraculous twenty-four hours out of the water, it will die in an hour if it doesn't come up to the surface to take in air through its mouth. This behaviour gives the pirarucu an advantage over the smaller fish they prey on, as oxygen is in short supply in these waters, particularly in the dry season. However, this advantage over their prey puts them at a disadvantage from their own predator – us. Tapioca is an expert pirarucu fisher. He explained to me that to catch the fish you need to lie in wait as it comes up for air about every fifteen minutes. It will often use the exact same spot to surface, especially if it's in the process of courting, which begins at this time of year.

Silently Tapioca paddled us round the beautiful forest, listening for the iconic splash of the pirarucu's breach and gulp. After several unsuccessful stalks, we saw an especially big ripple coming from some point hidden in the foliage. After silently approaching the source and waiting with harpoon at the ready for fifteen minutes, we started to move on to new waters, assuming that it had been scared off. Then, just as we left our ambush position, it breached exactly where we'd been waiting. Damn.

Later in the day we paddled back to the point where we'd heard one of the majestic fish surfacing. Once again Tapioca waited, alert with harpoon held high, where he thought the fish would surface again. The slightest movement in the

LEFT: Bruce joins Jorge Tapioca in a bid to catch the pirarucu – the largest scaled freshwater fish in the world

BELOW: Tapioca mending his nets after a day of fishing. Nets need constant maintenance as they are torn to shreds by caiman and piranha when left underwater for any period of time

PREVIOUS PAGE: Stilted houses line the banks of Mamirauá Reserve. Water rises about fifteen metres during the wet season

RIGHT: Bruce contemplates the water after a day of fishing. Despite Tapioca's skill, the pirarucu still elude capture after days spent pursuing the giant fish

PREVIOUS PAGE: A small canoe is transported to the *várzea* forest. Silence and stealth are essential to pursue the pirarucu through densely vegetated, flooded forest

dugout would give our game away and my bum was already completely numb from hours of sitting. I found it almost impossible not to reposition myself in the tiny canoe, so it astonished me that Tapioca stayed still holding a heavy harpoon in his raised hand for over ten minutes, without even the slightest quiver.

We were totally silent and I was tense with anticipation, but as we waited one of the fish we'd caught earlier flapped the last of its death throes, turning the hull of our dugout into a drum and ruining any chance we may have had.

Tapioca finished off the small fish by deftly smacking it against the boat, but we didn't see any signs of the lurking pirarucu after that. It's not the best time of year to catch pirarucu because the rains mean the lakes have flooded into each other, so rather than being confined within a small lake, the fish are swimming all over the forest and they're hard to pin down.

15 March. Jarauá

I'm sitting on board the *Spectrum*, and the beautiful river dolphins known locally as boto are playing just in front of the boat. They're considered rare but I've seen at least three pods a day since arriving in this area, often noticing them first by their distinctive and surprisingly loud exhalation. They're incredible animals – pink in colour, some bright like flamingos, and others a greyish blush. Apparently the colour changes according to their mood, and they flush a deeper pink when excited.

16 March. Jarauá

It's Sunday today and we're in the midst of a storm of biblical proportions.

We've moved the boat towards the edge of the lake where we can better weather the downpour, and the sky is black with heavy clouds, obscuring the moon.

After we woke and breakfasted on the boat this morning, we went on land and wandered through the village where most of the community were in the Catholic church. We passed open doors where those not at church were watching different things on their televisions – Formula 1, football, kids' TV.

At Tapioca's house the television was on and the children and their cousins were running in and out. Tapioca described a bit of the history of the reserve for me.

When he was young he used to go out and kill every single pirarucu he could, either for eating or selling on, but the stocks of the village were starting to diminish and they fell so much that when a priest arrived at the community they were ashamed because they couldn't even feed him. Tapioca said that the priest returned with a scientist, who told them if they hunted no pirarucu for three years the stocks would

replenish. Tapioca didn't believe him at first but Dona Lourdes' husband inspired the community to give it a go, and sure enough, the pirarucu came back.

Other villages in the area also want to get involved with the pirarucu programme, and Tapioca and Manuel have gone to these communities to teach them to count the pirarucu, and encourage them to be aware of the stocks. For the sceptics, they're a far better advertisement for this type of conservation than the scientists, but the message is still a tough one to get through.

The first scientific activity here was in the eighties, when José Márcio Ayres, a Brazilian scientist from Pará, came to study primates, in particular the rare uakari monkey – a white-haired species with a bright red face (also known as the English monkey on account of its 'sunburn'). Ayres brought scientific interest to the area

and was key in setting up the reserve in the nineties. Right from the beginning he worked with local people as monitors and as co-researchers so they were involved with conservation from the outset.

This afternoon the priest of the community, Padre Volnei, came to the village. He arrived in a green and white boat, tooting his horn madly. Wearing shorts and a stripy T-shirt, with a wooden cross dangling on his chest, he walked the entire length of the village, chatting to everyone along the way. He has been taking care of the Jarauá parish for seven years and knows everybody's name despite relatively few annual visits.

In the evening we went back to the boat, ready for the skies to open for this tremendous storm.

ABOVE: As well as providing an important environment for endangered species, the lakes of the reserve are an expansive playground for *ribeirinho* children

17 March. Jarauá

My thirty-ninth birthday today. Everyone has been lovely, wishing me a happy birthday, and we're going to celebrate in a couple of days when we have some time off.

Early this morning, Padre Volnei took mass in the village and christened three young children. His sermon was gentle and he spoke of loving your neighbour whatever their beliefs. In heaven, he said, there is no difference between Christians, Muslims and Jews, and neither should there be on earth. There was a great attendance and it was obvious he was extremely popular with the community.

After fishing all afternoon with Tapioca, I returned to the boat and, unusually, we all watched a film together called *Déjà Vu*, a ridiculous Hollywood blockbuster. Somewhat surreal but welcome escapism in the middle of the Amazon, and good to hang out with the crew.

18 March. Jarauá

We went out fishing today as a last-ditch attempt to get our prey before leaving. The sunlight fell beautifully through the trees, reflecting on the water, and we passed beneath strangler figs, under squirrel monkeys and past kingfishers darting through the branches.

Our quest for the fish was unsuccessful and Tapioca was a little disappointed. It's the hardest time of year to catch the pirarucu; it's much easier in the dry season when fish are concentrated into diminished lakes rather than the vast area of the flooded forest. I don't mind at all though because gliding through the forest has been like living out an Amazonian dream.

For me this shoot has been the most relaxing part of my trip. The crew's really chilled out, it's great staying on this boat and not having to move all our stuff all the time, and it's such a stunning environment. I didn't realize it before, but now I'm unwinding a bit I've become aware that the last three films have been quite exhausting.

20 March. On board the *Spectrum*, Mamirauá Reserve

Yesterday morning I said goodbye to Dona Lourdes, Tapioca, Manuel and the rest of the village. It's been fabulous to get some positive stories about the Amazon environment and I've really enjoyed my time with them. The whole community seem to be such a good advertisement for how conservation can work in this area of natural abundance.

Climbing back on board the boat, I was immediately greeted with a glass of caipirinha and a chorus of 'Happy Birthday' – this was a day off so we partied while we cruised to our next location. We've all been working pretty hard and it was great to completely relax with the crew. Playing our music very loud, we drank bucketloads of *cachaça* and celebrated life as we watched the forest go by.

Today I've mostly been in bed – recovering!

22 March. Mamirauá

Our boat has been steadily moving on for the last few days, and we've moored up near another community in the Mamirauá Reserve, but this one is not part of any management plan. I'm interested to see the difference between this community and Jarauá.

My first impression is that the village looks very different: most of the houses here are actually floating, built on rafts of logs, which are tied to something solid on the tiny bank. This community is on the Paraná do Aranapu, a fast-flowing river channel near the main Amazon River. Three years ago, the whole community had to move because land slid into the river due to the constant erosion of the riverbanks – this sent a wave along the river that was big enough to completely destroy the village.

ABOVE: After exuberant birthday celebrations on board the *Spectrum*, Bruce arrives at a second village in Mamirauá, which is far less involved in the work of the reserve

In this new location, Marina, our brilliant Portuguese assistant producer, introduced me to Branco, a *ribeirinho* she met on her recce. He invited me into his home to meet his wife Lenilde and their two children. The whole family were really excited to see us and our filming kits, and keen for me to move in with them while we film here.

This afternoon Branco took me to his field to pull up manioc – it's a very busy time of year here because it's when all the communities have to complete the harvest before the fields flood. All *várzea* lands are extremely fertile because of the annual deposits of nutrients in the sediment washed down from the Andes. But as with farming everywhere, the timing of the harvest is everything: too late and the crop is ruined by water; too early and the size of the tubers is insufficient to last the year. It was hard work digging in waterlogged ground in the relentless sun and humidity, but it gave me a chance to muck in with this friendly and gregarious family.

23 March. Mamirauá

Yesterday evening we met some of the scientists from the reserve who work in this area. Robin is a vivacious Colombian studying black caiman. There are two common species of caiman in this area: the spectacled caiman and the magnificent

ABOVE: *Ribeirinho* children playing at the water's edge. Three years ago the whole community moved because land slid into the river due to the constant erosion of the banks

black caiman, huge creatures that reach up to seven metres long. When mature, they are fearsome predators, hunting each other and mammals like the capybara (a rodent the size of a Labrador).

Henry Walter Bates, a Victorian scientist, wrote an account of his journeys on the upper tributaries of the Amazon; he penned a passage describing a man eaten by a caiman:

> *One of the men, during the greatest heat of the afternoon, took it into his head to go down alone to bathe . . . the man stumbled, and a pair of gaping jaws, appearing suddenly above the surface, seized him round the waist and drew him under the water. A cry of agony 'Ai Jesus!' was the last sign made by the wretched victim. The village was aroused . . . but a winding track of blood on the surface of the water was all that could be seen.*

RIGHT: Caiman feed mainly on fish, but there are accounts of them attacking large mammals

PREVIOUS PAGE: Manioc is a starchy tuber that has been cultivated and eaten in the Amazon basin for thousands of years. Correctly processing the crop is essential as some varieties of the plant contain deadly cyanide

These attacks, if they do still occur, are incredibly rare, but there are reports of caiman maiming people, especially children, on the riverside.

As hunting these animals for profit is illegal without an official management plan, it's also forbidden to sell their skin or flesh without a licence. Although there's a market for this elsewhere in Brazil from caiman farms, there's no market for caiman here and people prefer to eat fish. However, here they do catch and kill the caiman, in order to eviscerate them and use their guts to catch a species of catfish known as piracatinga. People hold the fatty caiman guts between their legs in the shallows of the water, and the catfish come to eat it, so they can simply be caught in the hand and pulled out of the water. Branco tells me that hundreds of fish can be caught at one time and then sold on, though not for a great price, and they usually end up in Colombian markets, where they are a delicacy known as *mota*.

Robin explains that the authorities of the reserve are fully aware that this is going on; he thinks a better management strategy might be to legalize the hunting of the medium-sized male caimans that are not breeding, and protect the rest of the species.

Tonight Robin and I went out on the river to find and collect caiman in order to monitor the population of the lakes. The water was dark and silent, and we swept our torch across the surface to reflect the red eyes of the caiman. Stealthily we'd approach them and then Robin would pick them up out of the water. All that we collected were very small – the length of a forearm – and we measured, marked, sexed and weighed them to gather data for his research.

25 March. Mamirauá

Branco and I went out pirarucu fishing this morning. There were massive water lilies everywhere, so big a child could sit on them. The air buzzed with insects and the water was still and placid.

Within moments of launching the canoe there was a huge splash. Branco stabbed at the water with his spear but missed. Pulling the harpoon out from the mud, he plunged the spear into the water again. This time it made contact with something underwater and it seemed as if the water erupted – I could just make out an enormous fish through the splashing. I held on to the rope attached to the spear and pulled the boat towards the roiling water.

Once we got really close I gained a good view of this giant fish. It had a flat forehead and a long tail, and Branco had harpooned it just under its dorsal fin. It flailed around in the water and Branco used his machete to slap it over its bony head as it became increasingly tired. Eventually we pulled it up on to the boat. The whole thing probably weighed twenty kilograms, so only a twentieth of the size that it can reach, but it still seemed absolutely huge, taking up half the space in the bottom of the boat.

Back in the village, Branco skinned the fish – the red and white scales are enormous and they can be dried and worn as large decorative earrings. Later today the village will share the fish, and we were also given a portion for the *Spectrum*'s galley – the meat is white, oily and filling.

This evening I was sitting by Branco's house and something caught my eye along the side of the bank. Approaching I saw four dead caiman. Even dead they are magnificent creatures, but one of them was already cut in half so the fatty innards could be used as bait for the catfish. I had a go at this strange method of fishing with a man on the riverbank, but I just couldn't get a grip on the slippery catfish when they came up to nibble the meat. Eventually I got the hang of it but in the time that I caught ten fish my fishing partner got about fifty. It seems a waste to kill both the caiman and the fish – if the village could harvest the caiman as part of a sustainable programme it could be sold directly. In parts of Brazil a square inch of skin can fetch twenty-five US dollars and this profit would mean the village would earn a lot more – enough not to have to kill the piracatinga as well.

26 March. Mamirauá

Today I moved into Branco's place and went out to collect wood with his family. There were incredible vines hanging from the trees, and the kids started to mess around

LEFT: This giant fish weighs in at twenty kilograms, which is only one twentieth of the size that the species has been known to reach

PREVIOUS PAGE: At last! After days on the water, Bruce eventually gets a close look at a pirarucu when Branco catches the fish with a harpoon

on them, swinging about upside down, doing proper Tarzan-style impressions, that sort of thing. The first kid made a good attempt but became unstuck when trying to turn upside down; the second smacked directly into a tree and the third went for an upside-down-and-backwards swing and slipped down the vine immediately. I joined in, then we all swung around wildly on the vines – the kids are tough, strong and happy and we were all shouting with excitement. All the while, Branco's daughter was laughing in the background, wielding a huge machete and adroitly chopping wood.

This afternoon we intended to go fishing again but I could sense a little reluctance among the men. Eventually I asked them what was going on and they explained that Brazil were playing Sweden, so we all agreed to watch the football instead. The kids were cheering and chanting, 'Brazil, Brazil, Brazil!' and we all

CHAPTER 4 **CONSERVATION**

squashed together on the sofa as soon as the anthems came on. After seventy uneventful minutes, Brazil scored the only goal of the match and the children ran around the hut in excitement.

The rest of the crew came over in the early evening as Branco had arranged to go caiman hunting and had invited us along. Robin came with the crew and we formed a fleet of two boats, one with Branco and myself, the other containing Robin and the crew, who would follow us at a distance. It's a bit strange having Robin here, as he's a scientist working to protect caiman, but I think it's a forward thinking way of trying to conserve the wildlife and to co-operate with communities so as not to criminalize them, which would otherwise send their activities underground. There are very few ways for these communities to get cash at this time of year. Obeying the law would stop them trying to raise the money they need to live. The institute's view

PREVIOUS PAGE:
The confluence of
the Rio Negro and
Solimões-Amazon.
Sediment rich water
from the Andes meets
the translucent dark
water of the lowlands.
The two channels flow
alongside each other
before eventually
mixing some six
kilometres downriver

is that the community needs to be shown how to work with the environment and be brought into a sustainable plan. This far-sighted and empathetic attitude seems commendable but fairly risky, as it condones breaking the law.

We paddled silently along the edge of the Amazon. It was a beautiful starry night; all the constellations sparkled brightly above our heads and it looked like the sky was exploding around the Southern Cross. Very soon, Branco saw caiman eyes reflecting the light from his torch beam. We advanced slowly in the boat. Branco raised his spear high and crouched, poised, just above the water. We got close but the eyes submerged and disappeared.

Branco saw some fresh eyes reflecting through the undergrowth. These weren't at the waterline and as we advanced slowly in the boat I could just make out the shadowy bulk of a caiman, high on the riverbank. Branco stood up, raised his spear high and gave a powerful throw. It was one hell of a thrust and he found his target. The caiman charged into the water. I radioed the crew from across the river and they rapidly made their way to us as Branco pulled this amazing creature up and, with a cudgel, began to wallop it over the head repeatedly.

I've been close to animals being dispatched many times, but for some reason this felt different and more than a little grim. The reality was that this splendid creature was being turned into fish food for cash.

It was very late when we returned to the village and we left the carcass on the porch until first light when it would be hidden in the river. I couldn't help a slight chuckle when the tiny family cat slunk round the corner and nearly walked into the thing. The poor little kitten let out an alarmed squeal as it leapt to the side and almost landed in the river.

27 March. Mamirauá

The piracatinga we caught two days ago using the caiman meat have all been stored in the river in a big wooden basket; they've been kept alive, submerged together under the surface, and today we hauled up the catch. The water sieved out of the wood and a wriggling mass of fish was left, all of them splashing about on each other. We scooped them out on to a floating raft, took a knife each, and began to gut them. Once gutted, they were put into a box of ice. A few hours later a boat arrived to buy the stock – the fish would be stored in ice and transported to Colombia. The captain of the boat, although not actively doing anything illegal himself, knows exactly how the fish are caught, so he refused to even come into the village, let alone be filmed.

28 March. Mamirauá

We're nearly at the end of filming for this part of our journey, and we're travelling through the rain, heading downriver towards the confluence of the Rio Negro and the Amazon River near Manaus. This morning we said a fond farewell to Branco's community and took the chairman of the village with us to the place where the AGM for the whole of the Mamirauá Reserve was taking place.

Boats lined the bank and the atmosphere felt like a village fête, with tarpaulins erected and people milling everywhere, sitting around, eating and chatting. We were soon reunited with Dona Lourdes and Robin and a number of other people we'd met. The best news of the day came from the chairman who'd come with us to the event. It seems that, having wanted it for so long, Branco's community is at last going to be able to join a management plan and have a quota of pirarucu to sell every year. They've been preserving one of their lakes for years now and it is brimming with the giant fish. Now they can make some money, legally, by harvesting them, and work with the conservationists to learn about sustainable development. They are also earmarked to be the pioneers of a caiman plan too, but that is as yet unconfirmed.

This is such a wonderful and unexpected postscript to our time in the area. All the community have to do to join the pirarucu plan is to pay off a small loan they have borrowed from the reserve. As luck would have it, this sum was almost exactly the same as the money we paid them for their generous hosting. Having said that, I do know that they intend to buy a lawnmower with this cash.

These last few weeks I've enjoyed a tranquillity unusual on this trip. I've been able to enjoy the beauty of the Amazon and its unique wildlife and, most importantly, to experience a conservation model that seems to work. People here need to live, and their livelihood has to be their first priority. But what I've seen suggests that conservation in the Amazon doesn't have to exclude people and their economic welfare. Communities can benefit, wild species can benefit, and this unique environment can benefit too. This is surely advantageous not only for the people of the Amazon but for everyone the world over.

'The noise of the generators is deafening, the earth is scorched and everyone huddles together under tarpaulins for shade at any opportunity. There's little romance in this search for El Dorado.'

CHAPTER 5
GOLD FEVER

Bruce's journey continues with a mission to discover the wealth of the Amazon, and there is no better place to start than Manaus – the city responsible for 98 per cent of the economy of Amazonas State. Amid the city's shacks and skyscrapers, Bruce mingles with affluent urbanites before leaving the urban jungle for an illegal gold mine in the depths of the Amazon. Miners and other hopefuls have rushed here from across Brazil to invest in expensive and risky gold extraction, yet the resulting destruction of the forest shows that the price of gold is more than just financial. To discover the real expense of such environmental destruction, Bruce travels to a scientific research base where he ascends into the heights of the jungle canopy to find out the value of the forest to the globe.

In Manaus, Bruce is hosted by a twenty-eight-year-old with a personal fortune of over £1 million. Serious money first accumulated in the city when it rose to prominence during the rubber boom, but after the industry collapsed the economy of the Amazon dwindled. To reinvigorate commerce the government of Brazil established a free trade zone in Manaus, where manufactured products include computers, motorcycles, jet skis and electronics. A new breed of wealthy entrepreneurs emerged as a result but, unsurprisingly, the majority of the 1.6 million inhabitants of the metropolis do not enjoy such financial riches; the minimum wage in Brazil is equivalent to around £120 per month.

Those who wish to earn this wage in just a few days can try their luck at the Grota Rica gold mine near Apuí. The 'Rich Grotto' mine has been active since 2006 and became a destination of choice for thousands when a television channel described miners finding kilograms of gold. Grota Rica is one of many illegal mines in the Amazon, and is part of an Amazonian gold rush with a long history – Europeans first navigated the river in a vain quest for the promised El Dorado, the legendary Amazonian kingdom of gold.

The Amazon also contains iron, copper, tin, diamonds and uranium and it's been estimated that in ideal conditions Brazil could make up to $50 billion per year from rainforest minerals. Worldwide more than 80 per cent of gold is used for jewellery, but this adornment comes with a high ecological cost: it's calculated that one wedding ring (weighing 0.33 ounces) creates an average of 20 tonnes of mine waste, which includes heavy metals such as cyanide and mercury that contaminate the food chain. Equally importantly, mining in the Amazon leads to increased deforestation.

Left standing this forest has an intrinsic value. The Amazon Basin is estimated to produce roughly 20 per cent of the earth's oxygen and is home to an unmatched biodiversity. It's a vital component of the water cycle of South America, producing half its own rainfall through moisture released into the atmosphere. Cutting it down, or even reducing it, could lead to desiccation and drought. The forest has also sequestered carbon over centuries and is an essential carbon sink: burning this timber would release greenhouse gases into the atmosphere.

Deep in virgin rainforest, Bruce works with a scientist to measure gas emitted from the microclimate, sampling the air from the forest floor to the treetops. In order to take samples through the night Bruce strings up his hammock in the highest branches of the tallest tree, overlooking miles of intact canopy. In just twenty years' time this view may no longer exist. Although cutting down the forest might generate money in the short term, the scientific data collected here helps to indicate the value of leaving the Amazon intact for future generations.

BELOW: Bruce blasting slurry to find gold in the Grota Rica gold mine near Apuí, Brazil

RIGHT: The view from
a flight over Manaus,
the largest urban
area in the Amazon

PREVIOUS PAGE:
Facing a westward
sky above the Amazon
River, as Bruce's
journey continues
through Brazil

10 April. Manaus

A few miles upstream of the city of Manaus I arrived at a helicopter pad by boat in order to meet Antonio Neto, a twenty-eight-year-old millionaire and member of the Amazonian rich set. The landing pad is a platform in the forest, on the edge of the Amazon River. As I disembarked, a good-looking young man dressed simply in a shirt and grey trousers stepped out of the waiting helicopter.

Antonio, who prefers to be called Tony, greeted me with a huge bear hug and invited me warmly into the helicopter, welcoming me to Manaus with the promise of a bird's-eye view over the city of his birth.

As we ascended above the city, Tony pointed out the European architecture of the civic centre and the famous opera house, which was built during the height of the rubber boom. We flew over skyscrapers along the river's edge and Tony explained that after the collapse of the rubber trade the Brazilian government had attempted to entice industrialists to Amazonas by making Manaus a tax-free haven. Flying westwards, we passed over penthouse apartments worth a vast amount of money

and then over sprawling beach houses on the Amazon's edge. Turning back, we flew over the bustling port areas and run-down shacks, some standing precariously on stilts over the water.

The contrast between wealth and poverty that I could see from the helicopter has long been part of the history of Manaus. Even the name Manaus hints at oppression: it refers to the Manáo tribe, a group that used to live on these very banks before they were persecuted out of existence by an onslaught of war, slavery and disease. This, sadly, is true of the entire length of the river, which is why not a single original tribal group is left on the banks of the main Amazon channel.

Tony's enthusiasm for the city and its history is contagious and this evening, as I accompanied him to a party at the waterfront house of a friend, I could see that he was looking forward to introducing me to some of its people. The house was thoroughly plush, with an outdoor jacuzzi and a bar. A plethora of well-dressed and very friendly people were drinking and chatting outside, looking out towards the huge river, which glowed under a deep red sunset. We ate manicoba, an edible

delicacy from the east of Brazil, which is made with the poisonous leaf of the manioc plant. It makes the tongue tingle and numbs the mouth – I really liked it. Turtle was served but I was assured that it was farmed and from a sustainable source. Tony's friend, our host seemed, stereotypically, a bit of an ageing playboy, and had erected a go-go pole as a permanent decorative feature.

Since this film was mainly going to be about illegal gold mining, and as we were calling it 'The Wealth of the Amazon', Tony's friend's party seemed to be the ideal place to start. Manaus has a reputation for people getting extraordinarily rich while others in the city suffer huge deprivation and I was interested to see what these wealthy people were like before we hit the mines.

12 April. Manaus

PREVIOUS PAGE:
Bruce and Tony (in a football shirt to the left of the dancer) at the Boi Bumbá, a famous carnival celebrated throughout the Amazon

It's midday, I've had a few hours of sleep this morning and I'm feeling surprisingly refreshed after a whole night dancing in a nightclub with Tony and his friends.

Yesterday Tony took us out on the river in a beautiful wooden boat called *Freedom*. I thought our boat for Film 4 was pretty luxurious but this vessel was rather elegant. We sailed down the Rio Negro to fish; Tony's a keen fisherman, and mounted on his wall at home is a peacock bass weighing over ten kilograms. He's eager for others to appreciate the natural side of the Amazon too and organizes fishing tours of the river so that foreigners and local urbanites can learn about this incredible ecosystem.

On the boat Tony described the spiritual fulfilment he finds in the presence of nature and the great outdoors. He loves the river and talks of the lifestyle of its communities in a way that seems to imply that he is almost envious of those whose lives aren't cluttered up with material wealth. He's not naïve in his opinions, in that he is quite clear it's a privilege to enjoy nature without having to actually live from it, but he feels he has every right to be romantic about the Amazon and its beauty.

Televisually I found this phase of the trip quite hard. I resisted the temptation to question the lifestyles of these people on camera as I saw much of myself in some of them. Sure, much of the historical and contemporary wealth of Manaus has come from exploitation of the forest's natural resources, often at the expense of the very local inhabitants I was meeting on my journey. But Tony's family is typical of lots of the recent money made in Manaus, as they have made their fortune through manufacturing, in their case making fire extinguishers, rather than by exploiting the forest. In fact everyone I met with Tony seemed to be giving something back in some way.

As it is, Tony's family have bought an area of pristine forest and plan to manage it as a conservation area; he's passionate about the river environment and describes himself as Amazonian first and Brazilian second. I liked him a lot.

13 April. Manaus

Every Saturday there is a huge rehearsal in Manaus for a celebration known as the Boi Bumbá, which takes place at Parintins, further downriver. Some of Tony's friends are heavily involved in organizing the event, and yesterday evening we went to the rehearsal. It is a famous carnival held in June to celebrate Amazonian identity. It's loosely based on indigenous traditions but there was little evidence of indigenous involvement, which was sad, but I was led to believe this was due to financial rather than racial differences. The rehearsal involved competing dance teams, lots of beautiful girls wearing feathers and a man wearing a white cow suit. Somehow I ended up dancing with some of the girls on the main stage. Typical.

Today was our last day in Manaus, and this afternoon Tony showed me the 700-seat Teatro Amazonas, an opera house of Italian marble and French glass that was the crowning glory of the European opulence from the rubber boom. In the evening we dined with Tony's family. It's been interesting hanging out with such rich inhabitants of the Amazon. They've gone as much out of their way to be hospitable to us as any other community that I've lived with, and I'm really glad to have met them all.

14 April. Grota Rica

This morning we clambered, a little bleary-eyed, into a plane and flew south to a place called Grota Rica, which appropriately translates as 'rich grotto', a gold mine discovered in 2006.

On the way we flew over the Transamazonica Highway. Building of this enormous road began in the 1970s. The aim was to create an 8,000-kilometre road to bisect the Amazon and open it up to development and population. As the road was being built the government ran campaigns to get people from all over Brazil to come to this new, abundant land. Farmers came and cut down the forest in search of fertile land but many were disappointed because the infertile thin soils were ill suited to almost all forms of agriculture. As I looked from the plane window at the belt of cleared land around the road I recalled a telling statistic that 80 per cent of forest destruction happens within 30 kilometres of an established road. Truly the quickest way to lose the forest is to build a road, no matter what the legislators may say.

In the end, only 2,500 kilometres of the road was ever built, and most of this was never paved. Funds and the political will ran out, though there are plans to resume building. I feel it's useful to be a bit of a cynic about the motivations behind these huge projects – the largest ship in the world can moor at Manaus, and people have always used the waterways of the Amazon for trade and travel. True, roadways can speed up extraction routes and increase company profits, but they also vastly increase deforestation and environmental damage. Many people I met are questioning their real purpose. Increased profits look great on paper and they increase gross national profit statistics, but it's no secret that local politicians have close election ties with big construction companies everywhere in the world. Here, at least, many people are questioning where such profits end up, as they felt that they certainly weren't being invested locally. It was hard not to be drawn into such political conversations as the trip continued.

We touched down at the town of Apuí and set off on the road to the mine. It was hot, dusty and sweaty. The sun beat down on the parched, cracked earth. It was a huge contrast to the cool shade of the forest, and a reminder of the benefits that the trees bring to the soil.

The sun had set by the time we arrived at the mine. We ferried our kit across to a guest house, which had opened one month ago. In the doorway stood Russia, the landlady of the house, who showed us to our rooms with a broad smile.

I'm sharing with James, the director of the film, with whom I've worked before on numerous episodes of *Tribe*. In the room next to us, Raquel and Solange, our AP and researcher for this film, have hung up their hammocks, and two doors down are Keith and Zubin, in charge of camera and sound, who have formed something of a double act since they met on Film 4, entertaining us all in the process.

The doors of the room lock only from the outside, which has added more fuel to the rumours flying around among the crew that this is a knocking shop (although thus far I can see no other evidence for this). After we settled in we cracked open a crate of beer with Russia, who told us about the early days of the mine. People from all over the country rushed here on the promise of gold as rumours of riches circulated wildly. It was lawless back then and no one could stop the thousands of hopefuls from coming. Russia herself heard about the mine on TV, when a Brazilian channel reported opportunists finding kilograms of gold. She packed her bags, sorted out care for some of her nine children, and travelled across Brazil to Grota Rica with her other kids. She didn't intend to stay for long, just enough to make money for her family, and then she'd return to live with them all again.

LEFT: Russia, the landlady of the guest house Bruce and the crew stayed in at the mine

BELOW: Families and children live and work in the mine, usually following the man of the household. There are no schools for this 20,000-strong population

PREVIOUS PAGE: Destruction and fires along the road to the Grota Rica mine. Road building in the Amazon often drives deforestation

It was dangerous then, there were gunshots and murders. If you found a lot of gold you'd hope no one noticed. You'd keep it quiet, avoid suspicion and get out of there as soon as you could.

After the miners came the second rush – the shopkeepers, bar owners, clinicians and prostitutes. All mining here is still illegal and these days there's also a growing concern that the gold is running out, but according to Russia there's enough of the precious metal to eke out a living. You get enough to pay for a basic living, booze and maybe a girl, and then you're back at it, chasing the dream of the big find.

15 April. Grota Rica

Yesterday we remained on the edge of the mine, talking to the shopkeepers and the bar owners. Lots of these traders, like the miners apparently, see this place as an opportunity to come for a while, make a bit of money and leave. I'm not meeting anyone who seems to consider the mine as home. Today Russia took us over to the mine itself – a massive mud slick. We needed to walk on numerous planks to avoid slipping in the slurry, while around us, spattered with mud glistening in the sunlight, some chancers panned for gold in the slurry. But this soil has already been looked through once, and most of the gold has already been removed using a water pump. There's only a tiny possibility that gold will still be there. But that, it seems, is enough of a draw.

There is a form of hierarchy here. At the top, you have the landowner. He lets plots of land to whoever wants to rent them. These tenants (for want of a better word) are the gamblers. They have to outlay the expense of the plot rental, a water pump and basic food and salaries for a team of (usually four) employees – the *peões*. These are the workers and they do the hard graft, blasting the alluvial soil into slurry using high-powered hoses. The slurry is then pumped down a ridged, sloped carpet so the heavier particles, hopefully golden, catch on the ridges where it's collected every few days, sometimes using the deadly poison mercury to bind the dust and particles to make it easier to collect.

Of the findings, 10 per cent goes to the 'association' who organize the mine (and includes a cut for the overall landowner). Forty per cent goes to the tenant and the remaining 50 per cent is split between the *peões* as a bonus on top of their basic salaries.

16 April. Grota Rica

Today we heard there was a new area being explored for gold, so we followed our lead and met a guy called Caverna, a nickname meaning 'cave digger'. As a 'tenant' he has a team of four workers. Caverna took us up to this new area of excavation, where about four or five teams of workers were grubbing away like ants on the hillside. The noise of the generators is deafening, the earth is scorched and everyone huddles together under tarpaulins for shade at any opportunity. There's little romance in this search for El Dorado.

Later we returned to meet the association working to try and legalize the mine. With their 10 per cent of all gold found, the association can provide services such as mosquito fumigation (there's a lot of malaria here), replanting programmes and health care. At the moment there's a strong desire for the mine to be legalized because it's so precarious to invest heavily in this illegal source, which could be shut down at any point, and everyone wants to legitimately declare their earnings for tax to make their home lives easier.

17 April. Grota Rica

Today I'm employed by Caverna as a *garimpeiro* (gold miner) in his machine gang, working alongside Janis, Gugu and Negao, who are his regular workers. We clamber into a pit of red earth and grab the power hose to continuously propel all the silt towards a pump, which sucks up the liquid slurry through a pipe. We delve into the muck to get rid of the bigger stones, so that they don't damage the machine, and filter the miry water through a series of grilles. It's so hot we take off our tops and are soon caked in mud, like we're part of the moving earth.

After a long day's water-blasting it's usual to fill the pit with water to keep out scavengers, but between our finishing and the water level rising too high these freelances arrive. Their faces and hands are smeared with dirt and they shovel frantically at the corners of the pit, desperate to unearth just something in the few minutes before it fills up with water. Even though they don't rent the land like others, they are grudgingly tolerated.

Meanwhile, we go to the grilles, which have filtered out the particles from water. The grit from the barrel is taken to a waist-deep pool, which can be drained if anything is lost inside. The miners here start panning the grit from the barrel, panning, panning, panning until they get to the bottom, where the good stuff is. Caverna said that hopefully we'll get 100 grams of gold and sure enough, as we work down the barrel I see a golden burnish to the black grit. It almost shocks me that it is actually there. After it has been panned as much as possible, all that is left is an incandescent golden dust and gravel.

We returned to Caverna's house, a wooden open-sided shack, where his wife was cooking for all his workers. Caverna put our pot of gold on to the stove to dry it out and then, very skilfully, he blew gently across the top of the gold powder, so that there was no dust that wasn't gold. He put it on the scales and it weighed 107 grams. From this everyone was paid their respective cuts in gold there and then. It's not pure gold, as it hasn't been smelted. Despite working all day I said I wouldn't take a cut, which aroused a rowdy cheer and I felt that was a good credibility point for me with the team. I was pleased as I wanted to hang out with the lads a little more and they seemed happy as they went off with their bounty wrapped in paper. In monetary terms they'd made about US$80 for three days' work, which is a pretty good wage in Brazil.

18 April. Grota Rica

Russia, our main character here, is incredibly impressive. In addition to running the guest house (which certainly hasn't been used as a brothel since we've been here) she also has a mine of her own and runs a pharmacy. Like a lot of the people here she's a real entrepreneur: children used to get sick from the water so she's built a well and she pumps clean water around the community. In our society Russia would be celebrated for her business acumen and energy, she'd be an achiever, a success story and an inspiration. But it's not the case here; she's invested a lot but she could easily get turfed out with nothing if the mine is closed. Her eyes glistened with tears as she considered how much she stood to lose if that happened.

It's much safer here than it used to be but beneath the calm it's easy to detect an air of turbulence. The police are on a rotation and, according to some, a few do a bit of racketeering – take a bit of money here or a bit of gold there. Alongside this, the miners run their own vigilante justice, in which there are certain unbreakable rules. Apparently, if you are caught stealing you'll be executed.

This evening we had a barbecue with Caverna's team. It was a good chance to chat away from the incessant din of the generators in the pit. I asked what they thought about going into National Parks or Indigenous Reserves to search for gold and all said they wouldn't think twice if there was a good chance of finding some. They also said that although they did care about the environment, they think that all the mineral wealth of the Amazon should be exploited for the benefit of the nation. As Janis said, 'I don't have a college education, and this is the best way I can think to make a better life for myself and my children.' Coming from where I do, I found no words to counter this testament and felt that if I had been born here I may well do the same. I was reminded that 'environmentalism' is a luxury perspective that many don't have.

19 April. Grota Rica

Russia took us to her own mine this morning. It's quite a distance from the others, and she has about four or five guys working for her. Unfortunately, two of her water pumps aren't working, which is causing a lot of stress. In the rare silence one could appreciate briefly how beautiful the forest all around her mine actually is. We sat listening to the calls of birds and the sound of water trickling from a crystal-clear spring. You literally bear witness to the pollution: you watch this clear water go through the mine, pick up the sediment and become muddy and contaminated.

She dreams of buying a house where she and her nine children can live, where there's enough money for her kids to go to university and for her to train as a nurse. She's gutsy and tenacious, and she refuses to give up.

When we returned to the house Russia took us to a 'shower' for a lovely pregnant girl, who is very poor. All the women came and gave her their babies' old clothes and made her feel special for a while. There's an unspoken sadness in the air here. Although everyone is upbeat and friendly, nobody really wants to be here. Often it is like they are hanging in limbo, away from their families, depending on the precarious promise of gold. I question them about their difficult scramble in this muddy purgatory between worlds and they tell me they can't wait to get home.

In the bar we met up with Janis, Gugu and Negao again. I ordered some beers, but they wouldn't drink. Gugu explained why. He told me when he first came here he was an archetypal *garimpeiro* – making just enough gold to keep him wallowing in booze and women until he completely lost contact with his wife and children for over two years. Then he had a revelation. God came to him in a dream, and he realized that he couldn't carry on squandering away his life – he wasn't saving any money. So he got back in contact with his family and told them that he would make enough to provide for them and then come home. And that's what he is saving for. He hasn't seen them now for four years but after his early indiscretions he wants to return with a small fortune to make it up to them.

We all danced to *forró*, a double shuffle to the left, and again to the right. I enjoyed it. There are occasional moments of laughter here, and everyone is doing a good job of trying to live a normal life despite so much adversity, but I am finding no glamour in any of this gold.

20 April. Grota Rica

This afternoon we went to a beautiful waterfall with our *garimpeiro* friends. It's very rare for these guys to get even half a day off, but they love to come here

ABOVE: In the early
days of operations
at Grota Rica, a
Brazilian TV channel
reported miners
finding kilograms of
gold. Such finds are
now unusual, but
miners will generally
earn more than the
minimum wage

when they can, and swim under the cascade of clear water, because they find it so peaceful. If they found gold here, however, they told me they would definitely destroy this place.

It's bad, they said, but what else could they do? Janis was a logger before becoming a miner and I asked him whether he saw a day when things might be worth as much in their natural form.

'Do the minerals have to be dug out of the earth? . . . Does the tree have to go in a sawmill to be worth anything? . . . Can't these resources be worth something left alone in the forest?'

'Wouldn't that be nice!' he replied. 'But it isn't the world I know.'

Another barbecue this evening at Caverna's place. It's the only half-decent food we've found here other than our boil-in-the-bag rations we've been regularly eating. Caverna has gone to prison on more than one occasion because he's been caught taking gold from indigenous lands. He thinks that, compared to the deforestation caused by farming in the Amazon, mining is a very small problem. I asked whether he would go to indigenous lands again, and he said yes, without question. I'm finding this very hard to take. Nothing is ever black and white and it's difficult to

condemn those taking a risky gamble in order to make a life for themselves and their families, but it is hard when you know the consequences of such actions.

ABOVE: Miners need to invest in equipment to flood the pits. Such investment is a risky gamble as the illegality of Grota Rica mean that operations could be closed down at any time

21 April. Grota Rica

In this world of gamblers, there's one team that are the biggest chancers of all and I'm with them in their mining encampment on the highest hill in the area. Milton and his two partners, Roosevelt and Feliciano, are tunnelling into the hill to find gold. They've been digging the tunnel for about six months and they've got about sixty metres into the side of the hill. As yet, though, they've only found a tiny amount of gold, and not nearly enough to make this gamble pay off.

Milton has worked with many engineering projects and he feels he has something of a Midas touch; he's done five of his own projects, and every time he has found what he's been looking for. He thinks there's about 300 kilograms of gold in the hill but, understandably, there's some anxiety and they keep a small mine on the side so that they can make a bit of money in the meantime. On a good day they cut into the hill another metre but it's difficult, it's potentially dangerous and they may never strike lucky.

Like Caverna, Milton has also been locked up for looking for gold on indigenous lands. He said that he had been completely ignorant of the threat of taking diseases into indigenous areas, but once he knew he vowed never to work on their lands again. I wished I'd asked Caverna whether his hard line was based on ignorance too.

Milton and the other two guys used to be married but, in their years of searching for gold, they've all lost their wives. Milton, a religious man, feels that the quest for gold runs in his blood. Even if he got really rich, he says he could never give up mining. Paradoxically, for him, gold is mystical and intoxicating, but useless. Humans have always lusted for it, scrabbled after it, and destroyed lives and environments for it, despite the fact that, in Milton's words, it's only for the kings and queens of the world to show off their wealth.

According to these guys the biggest problem here isn't their type of mining, but the big corporation gold mines, which basically make all the money and create the majority of the environmental damage. They perceive that all that money leaves Brazil and goes to the wealthy countries in Europe and North America, whom they view as colonial exploiters. They feel that theirs is a minor disturbance in comparison.

22 April. Grota Rica

After waking up in the *garimpeiros'* hut, I went to join them in their tunnel. Approaching the hill I felt a sense of jeopardy, as I've seen the gruesome images of mining disasters, but when I wandered into the darkness it felt quite safe. Even though this earth is liquefied slurry when it's hosed, it gives a good solid wall and the miners have boarded it up pretty well.

I followed Milton with a night vision camera. Chipping away at the wall is pretty easy, but the difficult work is shovelling all the mud chippings into the wheelbarrow in such a confined space, and then wheeling the barrow back along the single plank of the mine tunnel. There's a bit of a problem with oxygen but, as long as people walk up and down the shaft pretty often, enough air is exchanged with that outside.

Later today we were going to see Pele, a man I met briefly yesterday, because he's apparently found more gold here than anybody else. On our way to see him we heard that he had shot someone this morning. Apparently he had lent some guy money, which was never paid back. After an argument this guy insulted Pele's wife and then pushed him into a pit. Turning to walk away, he didn't see Pele crawling out of the pit behind him. Pele pulled out a pistol and shot him three times.

We were told that this man was dying on the other side of the river. I went for our medical kit with James. As we headed out of our camp, more news came through that he'd been picked up by a car and taken into town. There were rumours flying around all afternoon – one that he died on the way; another that he was going to survive. The last we heard was that he'd got to a hospital alive but paralysed.

Pele had run into the forest to lie low, so instead of meeting him we went to meet the miner who was the very first person to find gold here. Mariano is a slim, sixty-year-old black gentleman. He wears rags and a forlorn look. Two years ago he and a friend were separately walking around the area when he saw a glimmer from a stream. Looking closer, he saw that the light came from gold granules among the stones and reaching into the clear water he brought out a handful of grit laced with gold. He and his friend agreed not to breathe a word and they went to a bar to hatch a plan. In their excitement the friend got drunk, blabbed a bit, and before they knew it thousands were arriving. *Damn.*

In the following two weeks Mariano managed to get four kilograms of the metal, which worked out in cash as forty-four times his annual salary – a lifetime's earnings in a fortnight. He has fond memories of those heady days, which he describes as a giddy rush of anticipation, riches and beautiful girls. Since then he's had some sad years. He was gripped with gold lust and he invested, perhaps unwisely, by putting more money into digging. It was like putting all your money back on black because you'd just got the jackpot.

We walked to the site of devastation and I asked him some questions:

'Does gold equal happiness?'

– 'No.'

'Do you wish you had never found the gold?'

– 'Yes. I wish with all my heart I had never found it.'

'What was it like here when you first arrived?'

– 'The forest here was like a paradise.'

23 April. Grota Rica

We decided last night that this would be our last full day here. We've heard so many interesting stories but yesterday's events exposed us to the dark edges of the mine. Many around here don't smile in our direction. Come night, there is a drunken and slightly threatening atmosphere. We all agree it's time to quit.

LEFT: At the end of a long, hard process miners are left with a precious handful of gold and gravel, from which they take their wage

PREVIOUS PAGE: Battling the odds, a recently cut tree sprouts fresh leaves. The miners' association takes 10 per cent of all money made in the mine to provide community services, which includes a replanting programme

24 April. Grota Rica

Today began with fond farewells as we left Russia. She was tearful and it was apparent that she'd like to be leaving here too. It was another moment that brought my life into stark contrast with that of my kind and fearless hostess.

As we left we took the boat to cross the river to where our vehicles were waiting. Here the river is maybe thirty metres across and is the colour of black tea, naturally stained dark by organic matter. James agreed that we should go downstream to where the mine rivulets enter this pretty waterway. Sure enough opaque water poured into a chocolatey pool in the river. Further down there were more streams pouring silt and effluent into the water and within a hundred metres the whole river was a milky brown. Visually the mine may be an eyesore, but in relative terms it's a drop in the ocean. Here is the real impact on the environment. This river will now never be the same again and every plant and animal downstream of the mine is affected by it. All the more so if mercury is being used.

1 May. LBA Research Centre

RIGHT: Harnessed and ready to climb a forty-five-metre tree trunk to take air samples from the canopy

I've been in the Amazon for six months and on my journey I have learnt so much from everyone I've met. So many different stories and perspectives on the Amazon, but they've mostly been quite localized to the immediate area each group of people are living in. Today, however, is my chance to get more of a detached and scientific view about the value of the forest itself, its worth to humans, but also as part of our global environment. We've come to the Large-Scale Biosphere-Atmosphere Research Base, a two-hour drive north of Manaus, where over a thousand scientists come to research in the forest. I'm brimming with excitement about getting answers to some of the questions I've had since I left the UK, and that have remained dormant until now.

As Janis said at the mine, it would be nice if the forest were worth something all by itself, without being chopped down or dug up. The scientists here are researching projects to see if this is the case or not. This is such important information. It is here that scientists can put forward evidence supporting a case that the forest is important to conserve for financial reasons, not just sentimental ones.

3 May. LBA Research Centre

I'm exhausted and exhilarated after spending a night in a hammock up an enormous tree, looking out through the Amazonian canopy and hearing the creaks and groans of the trunks, watching the leaves quiver like alveoli, and the branches rise and fall in the breath of the air.

RIGHT: Preparing
for the night in the
uppermost branches
of the world's
largest forest

PREVIOUS PAGE: From
the top of the angelim
tree, unbroken canopy
stretches as far as
the eye can see

I'm here because of Alessandro Araujo, a scientist specializing in micrometrology. His work is to research the carbon dioxide levels emitted throughout the forest. So with two arboreal climbers from the UK, we ascended a tree to take samples of carbon dioxide. We needed to take gas levels from the air at three different points along a big angelim tree that was about forty-five metres high. We tested the air half a metre from the ground, halfway up and at the top of the canopy. The aim was to take samples throughout the afternoon, through the evening and night and into the next morning to add to thousands of similar results.

The trees here, like all plants, use photosynthesis to trap energy from sunlight, and in doing so they remove carbon from the atmosphere and incorporate it into their biomass. Forests are one of the main carbon sinks on the planet.

We talked and talked and talked. Alessandro responded to my barrage of questions with a lot of detail. Too much for here and too much for my head at times, but there was one clear message: *the Amazon is worth conserving*. It felt weird to be told this. Somehow I felt guilty because I'd already come to this same conclusion alone and without any supporting scientific data. I realized that I was carrying with me this huge preconception. But then again, *of course* the Amazon is worth conserving. How could any of us face our children if we let it just be destroyed? Once gone it would be gone for ever – never to return, and evidence suggests that there is a tipping point of about 40 per cent beyond which the destruction will continue unabated all by itself. But here I am beginning to get involved in politics and economics. This is all very new to me in my TV career. I have always been aware that I am only a visitor. I'm no scientist or specialist; I don't speak Spanish or Portuguese; and I have a strong belief in not interfering with other cultures or nations. But I also have a heart and a voice and know that the power of information and persuasion is strong. This is my driving force at this stage of the journey.

Alessandro highlighted three main reasons for the importance of the forest to be left intact. First, it is an important carbon sink or storage which, if disturbed or turned to crops or pasture, would increase the release of greenhouse gases and therefore global warming. Second, it generates local rain and weather patterns, which if lost could mean colossal droughts over the very fields and crops that it's being destroyed to make way for. And also it is a cog in global weather systems to a degree that no one seems to quite understand.

These are all pretty good reasons, I think, and surely enough to make us all stop, think and find out more before continuing to destroy it.

Many believe that, financially, these potential disasters would be much more costly in damage repair and maintenance than any profits made by turning the forest into crops, pasture, timber or the like. But maybe the problem lies in the fact that the worth of the forest intact is somewhat intangible. Its worth is wholesome and there for us all to reap the rewards together. But at the same time this makes it much harder for individuals to take their cut and get rich quick. This is now the overriding thought going through my mind as I head out of Amazonas State and towards Pará State, where I hear that big business, politics and big money are driving the loss of the forest at a rate that is hard to believe. This final stage of my journey is going to be a very different experience and I am somewhat dreading it.

'Wherever you drive through this area you see Brazil nut trees standing alone in the grassland, and it's a sad reminder that the whole place used to be forest.'

CHAPTER 6 THE BATTLE FRONT

The final stage of Bruce's Amazon journey is along the easternmost part of the river, where he gets ever closer to the ocean. This area of the Amazon is the front line of an environmental battle. Cattle ranches compete for space with soya plantations; illegal loggers encroach ever further into the forest; and land grabbers fake certificates claiming they own large areas.

Wanting to hear voices from all sides of this complicated conflict, Bruce works alongside ranch hands at the edge of the forest before joining the environmental police on operations to find illegal loggers. He meets families who have fled to shanty towns after being evicted at gunpoint, and accompanies an anti-slavery unit to uncover the disturbing practice of slavery in the Amazon. Bruce then joins the protest against the damming of the Rio Xingu and here meets the Kayapo, who are the final hosts of his journey before he sails the last stretch of the river to the Atlantic.

Firstly, Bruce stays at a typically large cattle ranch in the Brazilian state of Pará. Ranching is big business in the Amazon, where there are three times more cattle than people. Brazil is the world's top beef exporter, shipping over $3 billion worth in

2006 and supplying nearly every country, including the UK. Land was first bought for ranching in the seventies when the military government sold chunks of the Amazon for development, but some ranch land is falsely claimed with fraudulent ownership documents.

False land claims lead to forced evictions and violence. In January 2007 there were 772 known victims of land wars in the state of Pará. Stolen land is also cleared using people forced into labour through debt bondage and kept as slaves, an appalling practice that Bruce witnesses at first hand during an anti-slavery raid in the state.

Bruce and the crew accompany IBAMA (the Brazilian Institute of the Environment and Renewable Natural Resources) on two days of raids, finding illegally logged species and illicitly cleared land. Enforcement of the environmental law is difficult due to the size of the area: there are just fifteen rangers in a territory the size of France.

Land disputes also extend to legal projects, such as the controversial Belo Monte Dam, a project that has been approved by the Brazilian government. Many indigenous people oppose the dam, which will flood their land in order to generate hydroelectric power for industry. Indigenous groups protested successfully against a similar project in 1989, attracting the support of Sting and Anita Roddick. But the dam is back on the agenda, with mining and metallurgy companies stating it will create jobs and provide a renewable source of energy.

The dam has vociferous opponents: environmentalists claim decomposing vegetation will increase greenhouse gas emissions, that migratory fish routes will face disruption and that there will be sedimentary pollution. Doctors have suggested it will increase the spread of diseases, and engineers have suggested the Belo Monte Dam will be one of the least efficient in the world. Amid these voices of dissent is the strong voice of the Kayapo, who refuse to move from their ancestral land.

The Kayapo are a powerful Brazilian tribe who inhabit a vast area of the Amazon. In 2003 their population stood at an estimated 7,096 people and they have a long history of contact. Initially the Kayapo suffered from the diseases and displacement that accompanied the arrival of outsiders, but in the last few decades their contacts with commerce and media have helped bring the Amazon to the forefront of environmental debates.

After meeting them in their forest home Bruce travels the final few miles of the Amazon. Once he reaches the Atlantic Ocean he has come from 6,800 kilometres upstream, from the source in the High Andes. Bruce has finally completed his journey: the Amazon, from source to sea.

LEFT: Bruce with Kayapo girls, the final hosts of his journey

12 May. Fazenda Vitória do Xingu

I've been at this cattle ranch near Altamira all afternoon. To get here we travelled westwards along the Amazon on the *Castello Gerdis*, a traditional wooden ship, painted red and white. We'd slung our hammocks up on the top deck as we passed soya storage depots upriver, and watched as the soya was loaded on to ocean-bound boats ready to travel the last stretch of the Amazon and begin a journey across the globe. It was a sign that we're getting ever closer to the Atlantic, and to the end of our expedition.

Disembarking at Altamira, we loaded into trucks and drove along dirt tracks to this cattle ranch of about 70,000 hectares, which has around 4,000 cows. Ranching is big business in the Amazon: land is cheap and so profitability is high, and the river provides easy transport.

As soon as I arrived I was sat on a horse in what felt like a matter of minutes, galloping over fields to round up cattle. The only real riding I have ever done was with the Mongolian nomads of the Darhad valley, filming an episode of *Tribe*. There I was on a sturdy little pony with a wooden saddle, but here riding is done in true cowboy style. I was given a whip and my steed was a particularly handsome grey of about fifteen hands.

Alongside me was Tony, the manager of the farm, and his team of ranchers, a group of great guys who gave me a warm welcome – but there was no time to hang around. As soon as we'd rounded up the cows we were running them through pens, vaccinating them and treating them for ticks. This particular farm is a holding centre where the cattle are held before they're exported. They get fattened up because the pasture is so good, and then they disappear on barges along the Amazon.

This evening I headed into the nearby town. I'm not staying with any of the ranch hands because they all live in different places. The crew and I had planned to set up camp but there's no water so we've left the ranch and found a guest house of sorts.

13 May. Fazenda Vitória do Xingu

Today we woke early for a sunrise start at the ranch. I was helping the cowboys inoculate the calves rather than the grown beasts we vaccinated yesterday. It's a bit more physical with the calves: you herd them into an open pen, pick your animal and rugby tackle it to the ground. It's great fun. I was pretty hopeless at manhandling them at first, and weathered a few blows from their flying hooves.

I was being shown up by some of the young lads who seem, even at the tender age of ten, to be accomplished cow-wrestlers. After a few attempts I decided that despite being absolutely covered in cow shit I needed to get a little more stuck in.

I saw that the best technique was to grab the head and bring the cow down to the ground, where I'd pin the beast ready for the guys here to inject and brand it. I'm enjoying the company of the ranch hands. After this very muddy day of work we joined them for an excellent meal of grilled meats, which was quite possibly the best food of the journey to date.

14 May. Fazenda Vitória do Xingu

Another day on the ranch with Tony and the guys. The crew filmed some beautiful slow-motion footage of the stampeding cattle, which we showed later to the men on the farm. It's fun here but as always there's an underlying serious reason for our presence, which is to find out the stories behind some of the issues affecting the Amazon. Cattle ranching is the biggest use of deforested land, so the story of this ranch, and others like it, is a big part of the battle for the Amazon.

'Battle' is an appropriate word because the root of so much of the deforestation in the state of Pará (where we currently are) is illegal land grabbing, which is often violent. Land grabbers here are known as *grileiros*, from the Portuguese word for cricket. It refers to the practice of placing fake ownership documents in a drawer full of crickets, who soften and wear the parchment of the falsified certificates to make them appear aged. In addition to these *grileiros*, who claim ownership of uninhabited land, there are groups of *pistoleiros* – a name that's easy to translate – and it's not uncommon for these groups to force individuals or even whole communities off land with the threat of violence or death. The murder rate in the state of Pará is high, and all too often this type of land dispute is involved.

There is another particularly unsettling part of this process: once forested land is claimed, enslavement is often used to clear the area. It's done through debt bondage: people are brought across Brazil on the promise of a job and a wage but when they arrive they're informed that it cost a huge sum to bring them here, and that they'll need to work for a prolonged period to pay it off. They're engaged in the illegal and incredibly strenuous task of clearing the forest. It's a well-documented form of modern-day slavery and we're hoping to investigate it later in the journey.

Ranching is a part of this process because at the end of it all the land is bought as grazing pasture. The Amazon is destroyed but money gets made through the wood and then cattle, which is the driving power behind this whole insidious business of land grabbing and slavery.

LEFT: Brandishing an adult iguana caught without dismounting, this young ranch hand displays the skills of an expert cowboy

16 May. Fazenda Vitória do Xingu

It's midday and I'm sitting in the cool of the farmhouse. Yesterday I met Senhor Assis, the owner of the farm. He has four farms, each of a similar size to this one, so he's a big landowner but by no means the biggest in the area.

Like many other people in the Xingu region, he was brought here in the 1970s by the military regime. The policy then was to try and populate the Amazon by any means. One such project was the infamous Transamazonica Highway. Assis described himself on arrival as an ignorant peasant without education who was given a bit of land by the government and made a bit of cash. As was common practice, he used this to buy up some more land so that he could avoid paying tax on the money. This process continued and continued until he accumulated a large area.

Interestingly Assis said he now regrets cutting down the forest but he agreed that such sentiments are a privilege of success and not so easy for those still trying to make a living at the bottom of the ladder. He said that nearly all his land was obtained through illegal documents, which was an amazing confession. He also said that he wants to replant trees and give something back in some way. I believed him.

This last phase is going to test me a little because I know that I will see some terrible things here in Pará State if my research is anything to go by. But, as ever, I'm only meeting lovely people on my journey. If there are truly bad people involved in all this destruction, I'm certainly not encountering them. The farm manager, Tony, and the ranch hands have welcomed me wholeheartedly and all have offered us their friendship.

17 May. Altamira

Yesterday we left the farm and headed back into town in order to meet IBAMA, the Brazilian environmental police. It's the job of these guys to enforce environmental law and today we met Scapari, the head of the unit, and went out with his team in vehicles looking for environmental offenders, of which we know there are very many around here. IBAMA normally get their information from anonymous tip-offs, usually people who are concerned about the environment, as many of the people of Pará State are law-abiding citizens who don't condone the behaviour of the significant few who make money from activities like logging.

We took the IBAMA vehicles across the Rio Xingu, a southern tributary of the Amazon, by barge and arrived at a sawmill. There wasn't much going on there initially but while we were wandering about, one of the IBAMA team yelled at us from the entrance. A lorry loaded with huge logs was arriving. The logs had been

loaded so that the really expensive ones were hidden amid all the rest: right in the middle was a smaller trunk of Jatoba wood, which, like a few other hardwood species, is completely illegal to fell. In theory you go to jail if you're caught with one of these. Once the timber is processed, a log of this size could be worth over US$10,000.

The drivers, who were very relaxed and seemed totally unruffled by the disturbance, told Scapari and his team where the wood had come from so we sped away along the dirt roads from Altamira. Once we arrived at the alleged logging site we met the chap who had been in charge of the trucks. It all seemed very convoluted. He explained he was the manager of a sustainable development park and suggested the lorries were loaded at night, claiming he'd been unaware of any illegal activity.

He took us to the plots of legally logged wood on his reserve and most things seemed in order, but there were some irregularities with his paperwork. We followed a few leads, speeding around these muddy tracks trying to catch up with this person or that person. It took all day. Scapari managed to gather some bits of information but the investigation will have to continue.

I sat with Scapari after our chases through the forest. He has fifteen staff, and an area the size of France to control. Logging and land grabbing is going on everywhere and, as I learnt today, it's not just a question of catching people, but of tracking all the paperwork and forcing each individual case through layers of complicated bureaucracy. It's often impossible to legally prove that people are doing anything wrong. Even if you are taken to court, found guilty and fined, the fine is scrapped within five years. So, unsurprisingly, most people don't pay the fines. It was sad to see that no one here seemed to feel particularly threatened.

Scapari cares. His job is dangerous and he's not a popular man. But his attempts, however valiant and important, are a drop in the ocean. He didn't say that himself – he's a government agent and he didn't complain. Land ownership here is so complicated even before it's mired in corruption and fraud. It's almost impossible to determine who owns what.

At the end of the day IBAMA went and closed the sawmill and they held the vehicles loaded with the illegal logs – pending further investigation. No one knows how long that is going to take but it certainly won't be a simple case.

18 May. Altamira

Today was our second day with IBAMA. We went out in the helicopter, following another tip-off about four locations miles away on the Rio Xingu. I flew out in a helicopter with Scapari, two very cool pilots from IBAMA, and Rob filming alone.

LEFT: Encountering a convoy of trucks carrying illegally logged timber in the forest edge. Complicated legal processes mean that prosecutions for such environmental crimes are difficult to carry through

Flying over the area of the ranch we could see that the whole region was completely felled. Just miles of fields seemingly stretching out for ever, mostly grassland for cattle pasture. As we moved further away from here we came to the new forest frontier. From the window of the chopper you could see this logging going on everywhere near the forest edge. We didn't see any people, no one actually wielding a chainsaw, but all over the place were unauthorized roads, clear felled areas, straight lines cut through the jungle and logs strewn over the landscape. It was a harrowing sight.

Flying over the Xingu, we spotted a barge loaded with illegally felled logs. Immediately our pilot, who was incredibly skilled, lowered the helicopter and let it hover like an insect above the barge until it finally dropped down and landed on the barge itself. Over the headphones he told us to stay put because it was very possible that the crew of the barge might be armed.

As it turned out the guys on board were, again, very relaxed and friendly. They came and offered us ginger tea, which was not the reaction we had been expecting from those caught red-handed committing a serious offence. The barge was just full of logs, many of which were species that are completely illegal to fell. The boss, of course, wasn't there.

At first Rob and I thought we were extremely lucky to get such good footage of allegedly illegal activities in such a short filming time period. But then it dawned on us that, in fact, everywhere you look there are illegal activities going on and we were missing much more than we were getting. I suddenly became quite depressed as it was impossible to get a handle on how it could all be stopped. The efforts made seemed akin to a few people sticking up their hands to stop a tidal wave. It's vital that there are people ready to stick their hands up in the first place, that's the first step, but to stop this much more is needed – a lot more money and a change in the bureaucracy and law. My experiences with IBAMA have given me a real indication of what a very difficult task it is to enforce the environmental laws of the Amazon, but also just how brave and determined the people trying to do it are.

20 May. Altamira

Today we went to visit some people living in a community of stilted houses in an area outside Altamira. These families are the victims of land grabbers – they'd been told, by armed strangers, that they must immediately leave the land where they used to live or they'd be shot. Understandably they fled, leaving everything behind, and they ended up here on the edge of Altamira, where the community has regrouped.

RIGHT: More illegally felled hardwoods, a widespread occurrence in the eastern Amazon

On arrival I met Herculano and his family. Herculano is a wanted man. He has a price on his head because he's beginning to take political action against the people who forced him away from his home. He's only just realized that he might have some rights to fight back, so he's starting the legal battle, but whenever he returns to his land, he's surrounded by men threatening to kill him. He's one of the many people in the Amazon who are victims of the gangs of *grileiros* and *pistoleiros*.

Herculano's description of his ordeals reinforced my impression that land grabbing is linked right up to the big landowners. *Pistoleiros* come and force people off the ground; then in come the loggers, who take away the wood to the sawmills (who can make a lot of cash); and thereafter gangs of slaves are brought in to clear the area. After that the land is bought up by big farm owners, often as a means to avoid tax, and it's then used for ranching or soya plantations. Some of the richest people in Brazil, and actually in the world, have obtained their land like this. Judges and politicians are thought to be involved. Everyone tells me that the whole system is fraught with corruption.

Sadly, the victims of all this are people like Herculano and his family. He's been robbed of his land and his ability to fish, hunt and plant crops. Just as importantly

he's been robbed of his dignity. He's left here, in a slum, living under a death threat with no legal paperwork. He's not even safe here, because it's expected that soon this community is going to be forced to move again due to a damming project; because he doesn't live here legally, he'll get no compensation.

It's a human rights issue, and there are a few concerned parties in Brazil that have taken up this story – a bishop and some lawyers. But on the most part this is a story that is ignored.

We took the whole beautiful family out for a meal. The kids loved it so much. I felt very much for Herculano in this desperately unfair situation, and I can see no reason why this is happening to him other than ignorance and greed.

21 May. Altamira

We travelled back into Altamira and the town had suddenly changed. Lots of other British and Americans had appeared and there were other film crews present. Today a thousand indigenous people have arrived for a rally against the damming of the Rio Xingu. It's the largest gathering of indigenous peoples in the last twenty years. Coaches have come in from along the entire length of the river, bringing tribes like

ABOVE: Living at the water's edge in riverside shacks, families of this displaced community face death threats if they return home

LEFT: These boys have been forced from their Amazonian home by *grileiros* – illegal land grabbers

the Kayapo and the Ikpeng, as well as *ribeirinhos* and *coboclos* who have come to join the protest.

The project proposes damming the Xingu at several points along its length – it's a project that has gone through many different transitions but it's been running for over two decades. Sting and Anita Roddick protested against it in 1989 when they gave their voices to the Kayapo cause, but stages of the project have now been forced through by President Lula da Silva's administration.

Environmentally it's bad news. Flooding increases greenhouse emissions and destroys the forest, and dams prevent fish from reaching the headwaters of the Xingu to spawn. Ecosystems will change and fish species will decline, which will have a huge effect on the health and wealth of the communities that live on the river.

Furthermore, flooding areas means that thousands of people will have to leave their land with little or no compensation and sometimes not even any consultation.

This particular dam will provide electrical energy for some proposed aluminium works. Electricity has been promised to local people too as a pay-off, although since the industrial plants require a constant energy source it's unlikely that local people will benefit during the dry season. Again it seems that the people who are the most affected negatively will get the least, while all the profit goes to big industries and the few who support them.

We watched the protesters getting out of their coaches. It was a colourful parade of beadwork, feathers, banners and body paint, but you can tell from the determined expressions and angry faces that this is no celebration. I'm looking forward to finding out more at the meetings tomorrow.

22 May. Altamira

Today was the first day of discussions between the indigenous peoples and the relevant companies. The Kayapo arrived carrying knives or machetes, which is customary for many of these tribes when they leave their homelands. The chief engineer was giving a presentation and many of those listening took great offence at what he said. Things turned a little scrappy and a Kayapo woman cut the top of his arm with her knife.

It was big news and reporters clamoured to get the story. The Kayapo I met were unrepentant on her behalf. They said they'll fight to the last man for their land. They'll die for it.

23 May. Altamira

Yesterday's incident has generated a load of news and publicity, and most of the coverage has had a negative spin for indigenous peoples, describing them as violent, with one newspaper likening them to animals. It's a terrible shame because there is a very serious issue behind this protest, and again it's one of human rights being overridden in the name of 'progress'.

I found it a real eye-opener to talk with some of the people here. Bishop Kräutler, for example, has an enormous price on his head as well as three bodyguards due to his continuous public stance against the abuse of people's rights. An engineer from the University of São Paulo said the dam would be inefficient and wouldn't create the energy needed. I also met a Kayapo man called Pedro Paulo who, like the rest of the tribe, looked dressed for war – brandishing a machete and carrying bows and arrows. I asked his permission to stay with the Kayapo for the final phase of my journey and he said they would love to see us.

24 May. Marabá

After leaving the protest at Altamira we headed to Marabá, a day's journey along endless grassy fields which only recently were pristine forest. Arriving here we were told that every weekend twenty new corpses arrive in the morgue in town, having all met a rather unpleasant end. I'm told that the violence here is often due to land disputes, and I can well believe that after hearing the threats that families like Herculano's have faced.

25 May. Marabá

Debt bondage is categorized by the UN's International Labour Organization as a form of slavery. It has been perpetrated ever since other forms of slavery were abolished, especially in remote areas such as the Amazon. Con men known as *gattos* or 'cats' prowl extremely poor areas of the impoverished states in Brazil and tempt desperate men into travelling many miles from their homes with promises of decent work and pay. On the way they're deliberately stalled for a while, and when they finally get to start their work they're charged with their food, travel and accommodation, which often amounts to many weeks of work. That, followed by the extortionate prices for food which they can only obtain from the monopoly supply of their keeper in such remote areas, means that effectively they can never pay off their debt and are enslaved in work for the duration of their lives. Sadly many of these workers are so humble that they

LEFT: Leaving the largest indigenous gathering in the Amazon in recent years by boat, families travel back along the Amazonian tributaries to homes they could soon lose

ABOVE AND RIGHT:
Kayapo children are
endlessly engaging

PREVIOUS PAGE:
Two Kayapo men
atop Beautiful Hill,
at the edge of their
forest territory

don't even realize it is a deliberate con, and they are ashamed of their debt, working for many years as almost free labour. Some do try and escape but there are numerous instances of them being beaten up and deserted without pay or even killed.

Luckily the mobile force of the anti-slavery unit is having some success in reducing such crimes, and it is they who we are meeting today.

Our raid location is kept a secret until the last possible minute and soon we're off in a convoy of six four-by-four pick-ups. Our destination is many miles away, where we have a tip-off about a farm where the living and pay conditions are deplorable. On arriving at the scene there is rather a subdued reception by a few bedraggled farmhands. At first they're reticent to say too much, but when they realize that they are finally free and will be able to go home they all open up in turn. The wonderful mobile team are all busy taking statements and the stories are harrowing. One man is sixty years old and has been enslaved for forty years. His previous captor had beaten him up when he'd asked for pay. We have a look around: the living conditions are squalid and, as ever, there is no sign of any bosses or owners.

1 June. Krinu

Today began with a long drive past mile after mile of grassland sparsely populated by cattle and a few farms. We eventually arrived at the Kayapo village of Krinu. The town is only a few years old and it's right at the edge of their reserve. One of the reasons they have moved here is to fight against the encroachment of farmers on their land.

I met Pedro Paulo again but this time in a domestic setting, and his demeanour was far gentler than during the protest in Altamira, when he was in warrior mode. It was fantastic to see him at home. The Kayapo are a very exuberant tribe, with a strong aesthetic sense. They decorate their bodies with black, red and white paint and adorn themselves with beads and feathers. The women all have an iconic V shaved into the centre of their scalps, which gives the appearance of elongating the face and forehead.

They are one of the most famous indigenous groups in the world. And unlike other tribes I have visited in the Amazon, such as the Matis and Marubo, the Kayapo have been involved with media, industry and commerce for a long time. They're incredibly canny and economically savvy; in the eighties they employed

ABOVE AND RIGHT:
Bruce's body is painted
with fresh genipapo
fruit and soot. The
Kayapo believe they
share attributes with
other social animals
such as bees, reflected
in the geometric
designs of their body
decorations

PREVIOUS PAGE:
Kayapo women shave
and paint the centre
of the head, giving
them a distinctive
appearance

white people to come in and take their timber, charging them handsomely in the process and so becoming rich.

In 1988 the Brazilian constitution outlawed all logging on indigenous land, so this practice ceased and they lost a major source of income. It was shortly afterwards that they made a connection with Sting and Anita Roddick, and were an important part of the movement that generated global concern for the Amazon rainforest. Now, along with a lot of other indigenous groups, they're portrayed by environmentalists as the face of the Amazon and seen as an example of a way to save the forest.

It's an accurate portrayal in many ways: the Kayapo have decided that their future is to preserve the forest and they police and safeguard their land. Without them, and other indigenous peoples like them, farming would certainly encroach further. In reality, however, they are a human community – they can live sustainably but they are as capable of manipulating their resources and landscape as any other community.

I'm pleased to be ending my trip with a tribe that have had such an interesting recent history. They're very well informed about the rest of the world – they've been on television and they've made money – but they've actively chosen to conserve their environment and community, and I want to know why.

2 June. Krinu

This morning my body was painted by two lovely women using fresh genipapo fruit mixed with soot. Over my torso and limbs they painted a geometric pattern of finger-thick stripes and then designed a matrix of thin lines across my face.

I played with the kids a lot, messing about with them – they are wonderful, beautiful and engaging. They poke my sunburnt skin, chase me, tickle me and giggle.

This afternoon we had some formal talking in the men's hut and then some dancing. I was asked to join in and was prepared for the occasion by being given a thick rope of beads to wear around my neck, a bamboo stick and an arrow. The dances all comprise stamping one foot and they taught me a load of them; it was great fun and went on through the evening sun until last light.

3 June. Krinu

Today we went to climb a hill. We dressed up again and my decorations were augmented with additional red paint and beaded bands to wear around my upper arms. Last night was clear, cold and starry and today was blazingly hot. We walked over open rocky ground and ascended the appropriately named Beautiful Hill. At

the top were extraordinary views all over the Kayapo land, which is still forested as far as the eye can see.

Yet when you turn in the other direction, towards land that doesn't belong to the Kayapo, there is virtually no forest. Instead the landscape is farmland. It's a real battle for the Kayapo to keep the boundary of their land intact but they don't hate the farmers at all. They know that if the farmers weren't here they would just be in the *favelas* (slums) of São Paulo, and they understand that they are just trying to make a living. Pedro Paulo described the outside world as a place that is largely about money. He thinks that the main aim is to get rich, and then people don't share this wealth, and that this is the root of the problem. He said that the battle they have is against the system, not against the people. It's against a system that values money above the forest, and wealth above happiness.

His words reflected all the things I have learnt. It seemed so fitting to hear them now on Beautiful Hill, on the forest frontier, near the end of this long and overwhelming journey.

4 June. Krinu

First thing this morning we had a festival to start the agricultural season. Everyone was up at about six, and we got painted up and had a bit of a song and dance routine. It started before first light – it was cold, and none of us were allowed to wear T-shirts so we all stood around the few embers of the fire trying to prove our toughness.

Then we jumped into two boats upriver. At first the water was very clear but after a confluence it became much cloudier, and the Kayapo said it was polluted from all the farms in the area – from the pesticides and whatever else is used. They can't drink from this river.

We were travelling to collect Brazil nuts. In addition to protecting their land, another reason the community moved here was because of the presence of the nut trees: they don't grow everywhere, but as clusters in one area. They took me to one tree, where the nuts have already fallen on the ground. The fruits are big, almost like a coconut, and inside are between ten and twenty smaller nuts, each encased in its own shell. When you peel that back you get to the nut that we recognize, which tastes amazingly oily and rich, very different from those I'd eaten at home.

There used to be far more nut trees here but last year there was a terrible tragedy for the village of Krinu when agricultural burning by the local farmers killed off nearly all of the Brazil nut trees in the area. The Brazil nut is important to the Kayapo as a food and income source but also as a symbol: the tree is iconic. In fact,

LEFT: Bruce, with Kayapo face decorations, walking up Beautiful Hill, where the Kayapo give him the final message of this overwhelming journey.

PREVIOUS PAGE: A Kayapo mother prepares cassava flour, which she will use to coat the strips of wild deer, to her left, before baking the meat underground with hot rocks

it is illegal to chop down a Brazil nut tree anywhere in Brazil. Even in the cities, shopping centres will be built *around* these trees to leave them intact.

The result of this is that wherever you drive through this area you see Brazil nut trees standing alone in grassland, and it's a sad reminder that the whole place used to be forest. Mostly these trees are dead, because the fires used to make pasture have killed them, but they are left to stand, skeletons littering the landscape.

6 June. Santarém

Last night I was honoured with not one but *three* Kayapo names. Names are central to Kayapo culture and naming ceremonies are very elaborate. We danced into the night with the whole village turning up for the occasion. My time with them has been short but its impact has been very powerful, and I am so pleased that the last words I hear from the Amazon are from some of its original inhabitants. We flew out by light aircraft first thing this morning from an airstrip near the village. As we rose above the canopy suddenly everything was clear. Once again, there was such a dramatic difference between the deforested pasture all around and the Indigenous Reserve full of trees. It was a vivid reminder that without people like the Kayapo fighting to save their land there would simply be no forest here at all.

8 June. Santarém

To finish our journey we have returned to the river itself for the last leg. It is still very much at the heart of my trip and I can only truly say I've finished when I reach the Atlantic Ocean by river. From Santarém to Belém will take a few days. During this time on the boat Rob is interviewing me to try and get a summary of my whole journey and a conclusion of sorts as to what I've learnt along the way. It doesn't quite seem real that my Amazon odyssey is now coming to a close. I have lived and breathed this vast basin and its wonderful inhabitants for the last seven and a half months; the thought of returning home to a normal life is a bit scary.

9 June. Belém

My journey is finally over. The ocean is in front of me and I find myself awash with emotions. On the boat these last few days Rob has done a great job of teasing out of me all the lessons I've learnt along the way. He took notes on my impressions and experiences before recording my final thoughts. It's been something of an epic and I feel more than a little shattered. There is so much going through my head and I feel for the first time in my life I am going to get a culture shock on going home. My

'normal' life will seem so wasteful and frivolous. I know that I need to decompress a little and allow the lessons to sink in slowly but right now I'm rather pumped up.

Back at the start of the journey I knew so many facts about where the mighty Amazon clashed with the mighty Atlantic. Geographically, it is fascinating. But somehow that all seems slightly irrelevant as I stare at the endless water. I now realize that it is the people of the Amazon who have affected me the most, not the natural features of the river. They have all shared their lives with me and taught me something new. They've contributed to a huge message which I hope to pass on in some way on their behalf: a simple message for us all, but one easily overlooked. If we continue to ignore it may well destroy them and their surroundings, and that would have drastic consequences for the rest of the world too.

EPILOGUE

Sitting in the departure lounge of Heathrow airport all those months ago, I remember feeling more than a little apprehensive about this expedition: how much would these people who live and work along the world's greatest river open up to me? How would I really get to the heart of their issues while being on the move so much? I'd been so used to immersing myself in other cultures for long periods of time, living with people and slowly gaining their trust until they welcomed me right into their lives, that this journey felt like it was going to be a huge challenge.

Luckily my first meeting, that with Gladys and Rodolfo in the High Andes, was very enlightening. Like nearly all the people we encountered after that, they were more than willing to invite me into their world, to expose their problems to me. It was a rich and also humbling experience: they reminded me that some of the poorest people in the world are among the most generous. Theirs was the first of many lessons.

With that wonderful start my journey began in earnest. As we progressed, the complexity of the issues at stake became increasingly obvious – and, in truth, overwhelming.

There was lots to be despondent about as I met members of the various tribal peoples who depend on the Amazon and its natural resources. Hearing first-hand accounts from the Asháninka of the atrocities of the Shining Path was a chilling reminder of the recent bloody history of the area. The battle between the Achuar and the oil companies highlighted the indisputable fact that big industries don't hesitate to destroy in order to feed the needs of the rich nations. And one of the hardest moments for me was seeing my old friends the Matis in the *Vale do Javari*. It

was deeply shocking to see how much they'd been affected by contact with outsiders, to note how many of them are dying from easily prevented epidemics.

And this was just the beginning. Everywhere we looked there seemed to be destruction in the name of *development* with little regard for future cost or real worth.

But, as ever, I found that not everything is black and white. As we dropped into the lowlands in Peru, Antonio and the coca farmers taught me that although they were directly involved in what *we* call an illicit trade, it didn't make them bad people. The loggers gave me friendship and an opportunity to dispel the popular demonization of the worker on the ground.

Our coming into Manaus gave me an opportunity to answer some of my bigger questions about the Amazon. It was here that I discovered the worth of this pristine forest and where I became convinced that the Amazon is indeed worth preserving in its natural state for tangible reasons, beyond sentimental ones. Sadly I also realized that, if things don't change, the whole Amazon Basin might one day be open farmland and pasture.

The will to improve the situation is there if you look around. For example, Mamirauá gave me hope for ways to sustainably conserve the forest while simultaneously providing a way for people to improve their lives. And we met so many officials doing amazing jobs in the face of a torrent of crimes and abuses, killings and death threats towards people who were simply getting in the way of the

money-making – such brave citizens and officials trying to fight the tide of greed, destruction and organized crime.

But my overriding feeling as I journeyed down the river was that it is the consumer who is just as much a part of the problem. The Amazon is only an example of what is happening everywhere round the world: a few people getting very rich while the world's resources are being inextricably depleted and the consumers remain largely ignorant of their destructive actions.

So until the whole world changes, what should we do? Well, if we want to preserve the Amazon we need to persuade those who live there not to destroy it, for all our sakes. Carbon credits and scientific evidence are a good way of incentivizing, and if it proves very costly we ought to remember where we got our own riches from in the first place. There is a good chance that the violations going on there will have an impact on other parts of the world too. No one knows for sure, but anyone who has listened to the experts would agree that the risk is too big to take a gamble on.

We should listen to the advice of the indigenous peoples rather than systematically destroying their land. If we don't wake up to what's going on everywhere, our children and children's children will one day ask us why we allowed all our natural resourses to be destroyed. Once upon a time we may have had ignorance as an excuse, but modern communications have changed that. It is happening, and nobody knows where the tipping point is. Together we have the ability to stop it. But only if we decide to.

ACKNOWLEDGEMENTS

Thanks to:

Alberto Labarello, Alex Elam, Alfredo Marubo, Alison Rae, Aliya Ryan, Almudena Parrado, Ana Claudeise, Ana-Maria Rivera, Andrew Mitchel, Andrew Smith, Andy Netley, Angel Mozombite, Antonio Neto, Apache, Bush Matis, Carolina Ramos, Cassio Camarada, Chicao Frasisco Ferreira Pinto Filho, Chris Moore, Chris Van Tulleken, Christina Daniels, Clare Pollock, David Ayers, Dionisio Alves, Dudu Edwardo Gomez, Elena Welper, Emma Haskins, Fabricio Zanchi, Felix Todd, Flavio Somogyi, Greg, Greg Proven, Gwynfor Llewellyn, Heron Alencar, Hugo Meirelles, Indios Tenherim, Ireo Kayapo, Isabel Soares, James Aldred, James Blackman, James Smith, Jane Houston, Jo Lethbridge, Jonathan Baker, Jorge Fachin, Julia Connolly, Katy Follain, Keith Schofield, Laura Santana, Leandro Balberdes, Leona Cowley, Leticia Valverdes, Liz Smith, Luciene Pohl, Luis Claudio, Luis Felipe Ulloa, Marco Lima, Marina De Brito, Mario, Matt Brandon, Matt Norman, Mike Page, Naomi Fidler, Nick Lowndes, Oliver Laker, Osman Brasil, Owain Elidir, Paul Saroli, Pete Brownlee, Peter Eason, Raquel Toniolo, Rich Moss, Rob Sullivan, Robinson Botero Arias, Ruth Buenida, Ruth Spencer, Sam Organ, Silvia Ciborowski, Solange Welch, Sophie Ransom, Steve Castle, Steve Robinson, Tania Sanaiotti, Willow Grace Murton, Xand Van Tulleken, Zubin Sarosh.